Peter, the only child of John and Margaret Hunt, was born in Brighton in July 1940, but at the age of five, began his life as a child in post-war Hong Kong.

At the age of seven this idyllic life was shattered when he was sent back to England to enrol in a Catholic boarding school in Sussex, and later a Catholic boarding school in Somerset. These years are covered in his first memoir, entitled a *Child of a bygone era*.

After University in Dublin, his next twenty years, the subject of this book, were spent primarily in London, through the 60s and 70s. He worked in advertising and marketing, including a year at Business school, then onwards to market for Jimmy Goldsmith, and later for the Jamaican Government and the world of Havana cigars.

He has lived in Jersey for the last 30 years where he has published six books about Jersey and has written articles for the local newspaper the *Jersey Evening Post*.

Running through this memoir are the women who had an enormous influence on my young life. I have lost touch with one, Hope (understandably) but sadly Annabel, Jacqui, Jane and Jenny are no longer with us. It is in their memory that much of this memoir has been written.

I have been blessed with some very good friends; John Hickmott, David Hemming, John Tackaberry, Carl Bontoft, Peter and Gwen Tory, the McConnell family, Anthony and Albena Robson and some delightful friends who were women that gladdened the down times in my life Kay, Audrey, Gail, Margaret and Val to name just five.

I must also thank my parents. To a degree, they sacrificed their lives to give me a good education and the means to live an independent, perhaps spoiled, life – the life of a colonial boy in London in the 1960s and 1970s.

Finally, for 22 years Jenni Voisin and her family have considered me as one of their own. Having never had my own family, I am sincere grateful for their introduction to a life I never thought to experience nor to enjoy so much.

Peter Hunt

THE GROWING PAINS OF A COLONIAL BOY

AUSTIN MACAULEY PUBLISHERS™
LONDON • CAMBRIDGE • NEW YORK • SHARJAH

Copyright © Peter Hunt 2023

The right of Peter Hunt to be identified as author of this work has been asserted by the author in accordance with sections 77 and 78 of the Copyright, Designs and Patents Act 1988.

All rights reserved. No part of this publication may be reproduced, stored in a retrieval system, or transmitted in any form or by any means, electronic, mechanical, photocopying, recording, or otherwise, without the prior permission of the publishers.

Any person who commits any unauthorized act in relation to this publication may be liable to criminal prosecution and civil claims for damages.

All of the events in this memoir are true to the best of author's memory. The views expressed in this memoir are solely those of the author.

A CIP catalogue record for this title is available from the British Library.

ISBN 9781398471344 (Paperback)
ISBN 9781398471351 (ePub e-book)

www.austinmacauley.com

First Published 2023
Austin Macauley Publishers Ltd®
1 Canada Square
Canary Wharf
London
E14 5AA

The journey by train and ferry from London to Dublin via Fishguard and Rosslare was made only acceptable by our own company. It was in September 1958 and I was just 18, my last four months having been spent in a halcyon haze of pleasure in the delights of a vibrant and exciting Hong Kong, home of my youth, my upbringing to this present point having been recorded in my book *Child of a Bygone Era.*

John Tackaberry, my other prop forward from our Downside school rugby days, and I were on our way to continue our education at Trinity College Dublin – an adventure definitely into the unknown. Not only had we never been to university, in those days still called university not uni, we had never been to Ireland nor Dublin. Unlike its English equivalents, Trinity Dublin's degree course was for four years, not three. We had already been informed that we would have to spend our first year in lodgings in Dublin, then two years in college and our last year back in lodgings.

Our first impression of the city of Dublin was not encouraging. We arrived at Westland Row (now Pearse) Street station and descended down the stairs from the roof top platform to Westland Row itself.

From there, it was only a short walk, hauling our suitcases, up Pearse Street to Trinity College and the porters' lodge but under grey, drizzling clouds from which the gentle but persistent rain seemed not only to permeate our clothing but also the very stones and streets of the city itself.

It was also bitterly cold.

We made ourselves known at the porters' lodge and carried on to the vestibule which opened out into the first of the college's squares featuring a striking campanile. The vestibule was full of notice boards asking for new students to join various sporting clubs and societies and how to find lodgings – something we obviously needed to do.

The imposing C18th classical revival frontage to Trinity College

Darkness was descending and John had arranged for us to stay our first two nights with his uncle, whom I don't think he had ever met, who lived out in an area called Inchicore. This was a tough area and one that was considered to be sympathetic to the Irish Republican Army (IRA) and antagonistic to the English. John's uncle Jerry owned and ran a shoe shop which was basic, to say the least.

The shop was at the front of the house, the kitchen cum sitting room at the back. Between the two was an ancient lavatory and basin. Jerry had an assistant called Mary who shared the house with him. The lavatory was basically for her use and should we wish to urinate, the back of the house had a tiny yard open to the canal, kindly provided by history for our use.

Jerry proved to be a kind and hospitable man who introduced us to the snooker club adjacent to his shop which had tables and a bar and which served us with Guinness, sausages and chips, all three of which were delicious.

However, it continued to be dreadfully cold and Jerry's house had no heating.

Returning from the snooker club, Jerry explained that there was only one large bedroom and one small bedroom, Mary's, but as it was so cold, he suggested that all of us including Mary sleep in his bed fully clothed against the cold. This we did and, perhaps because we had been travelling for days and had sunk quite a few pints of Guinness, we had a surprisingly good night's sleep.

The next morning, we returned to college, and made ourselves known to R. B. McDowell, the Junior Dean, at his office – an office which was not only the college's administrative centre but also the Junior Dean was responsible for law and order amongst us students. We then searched the notice boards and found a bed and breakfast establishment that had one room with two single beds for rent in an area called Ballsbridge, home of the Lansdowne Road rugby stadium, the RDS (Royal Dublin Society) showground, various embassies and roads of pleasant, genteel housing.

Close to the south of our college, its sports grounds and its medical school, the position was ideal for us and we moved in the following day, having had a fond and rather intoxicated farewell evening with Mary and Jerry. The strange thing about our brief stay with Jerry was the attitude of the Irish we met. We had understood that our English accents might arouse hostility, particularly in the Inchicore area. Not a bit of it; we were welcomed with what is described as Irish charm which it really is.

I say city but Dublin, in those days, though a capital city, was much more a provincial town centred around one area south of the River Liffey and one area north of the river. Its population was around 650,000 out of the country's 2.5 million.

We were later to discover how the town gave the impression of almost two separate towns divided by the River Liffey.

The north side's main thoroughfare was O'Connell Street, which ran north from the bridge over the Liffey, past the statue to O'Connell (the man himself, as the Irish would say), past the post office made famous in the 1916 Easter Rising when Patrick Pearse read out the declaration for creating an Irish Republic, past the site of Nelson's Column blown up by the republicans in 1966, passed the stately Gresham Hotel, favoured by the elite Dublin clergy and up to the Mountjoy jail.

To the west, on the banks of the Liffey, were the law courts, Kilmainham Gaol and Phoenix park, to the north Glasnevin and to the east, Howth; at that time, these were the furthest reaches of the city on route to the airport.

Behind the post office is Moore Street's market famous for its stallholders with their Dublin accents and Irish humour. In my day, the call I remember was "tuppence each the apples and oranges". It is a call that has never left me.

South of the Liffey bridge was situated the Bank of Ireland, Trinity College (TCD) and running down from them Grafton Street, the main shopping Street in Dublin, St Stephen' Green housing the College of Surgeons and the competing Catholic university – University College Dublin (UCD) and the two gracious Georgian Squares of Merrion and Fitzwilliam. To the west of this central area, were housed the Jameson whiskey distillery and the heart of Ireland's most famous stout – the Guinness brewery.

The areas further out included Ballsbridge, Rathgar and Rathfarnham areas where many students lived and many pleasant streets of elegant houses backed onto less salubrious areas.

Running south from central Dublin through the dockland area and by the Irish Sea were communities such as Sandymount, Blackrock, Monkstown, the port of Dun Laoghaire with further south the favoured residential area of Dalkey and Killiney – then onwards on the road to the south of Ireland.

To the south and west of the town, on the road to Naas, lied access to the beautiful Wicklow hills and the village of Stepaside which became one of our favourite haunts. I have to admit, we did not take much interest in Irish history, which is complicated to say the least, but we did appreciate that Ireland and Dublin had been left behind since the middle of the 19th century.

Since the Second World War, the country had been governed by the ultra-conservative Catholicism of the combination of two authoritarian national heads of state and church. The first was Eamon de Valera, Taoiseach (Prime Minister) from 1957 to 1959 and President from 1959 to 1973 and the second, Archbishop John Charles McQuaid, Primate of Ireland and Archbishop of Dublin from 1940 to 1972 – an enormous length of time for their domination of rigid conservatism. Their influence was only broken by their deaths, the liberalism of the late 1960s and the extraordinary birth of the Celtic Tiger.

A more dramatic result of this severity was the continual movement of youth away from Ireland. Between 1961 and 1966, 33% of men and 30% of women between the ages of 20 to 24 left their homeland mainly to England where jobs, wages and social services were far above Irish standards.

I have never quite understood the Irish catholic attitude towards women and sex at that time. It seems that women were considered mainly as virginal housewives or breeding machines or somehow both. For instance, in our day, all forms of contraception were banned as was any form of termination. Censorship of movies and all literature was heavily applied. I had a prized collection of first day issues of the first year of Playboy's magazine. I had sent it through from Hong Kong to London in my luggage and, without thinking, sent it on to Dublin. The twelve issues were impounded by Customs and destroyed.

Trinity was considered to be an anomaly by the Catholic authorities as it had been founded by Queen Elizabeth I to convert the heathen Irish to Protestantism. Over the following centuries, it had been at the centre of the Pale, the English governing heart of Ireland and many of its alumni had been Protestants, particularly its authors including Oscar Wilde and Samuel Beckett. However, by the 20th century, it seemed to us to have no particular proselytizing activities other than its on-campus chapel remaining Protestant.

Irish Catholics were banned from attending Trinity and were enrolled in its Catholic competitor University College Dublin, situated in St Stephan's Green. One of my contemporaries from Downside was from Cork. He had to apply for a dispensation from the Archbishop to attend Trinity, religious fervour was that strong and only received a dispensation because he had won a scholarship to Trinity from Downside.

This attitude meant that there were virtually no native Irish men at Trinity and, even worse, no Irish women. Women made up approximately 20% of the student body and were from the British Isles or Northern Ireland. They were not allowed to board in college, so lived in town. They had to leave college by six in the evening unless they had dispensations to attend specific social or formal occasions. They made a welcome contribution to our lives in college and vitalised such activities as the Players and social functions. Their sanctuary, known by some of us as the Dolls' House, was building number six in the front square.

As we came to know Dublin more, we began to understand its attraction to famous, even infamous, visitors and locals. I suppose we did not at first get to know many born and bred Dubliners other than restaurant and pub staff – that was to come later.

The town itself was a mixture of Georgian splendour, 19th century tenements, slums and various post-war developments but its great advantage was that it has the Irish Sea to its east, the Wicklow Hills to its southwest and the agricultural lands to the west and north.

One of my delights was to walk across O'Connell Bridge, turn left and walk along the Liffey to the Four Courts, then cross back over the river by the Halfpenny pedestrian bridge. From there, I could wander through the streets in a part of town that I did not often visit that encompassed Dublin's Town Hall and Dublin Castle as I worked my way back to Trinity.

Another delight was to drive up to the majestic Wicklow Hills, to visit villages such as Sallygap and Blessington, or Powerscourt with its house and world-famous gardens and my personal favourite, the village and lake at Glendalough. We could return for a pit stop at Delgany, or a walk along the cliffs at Bray Head and back to Dublin itself.

In town for our pleasure, other than pubs and restaurants, were two cinemas. The one most visited by us was the Abbey on Pearse Street. It had seen better days but featured more art type films. We visited the more comfortable Savoy cinema on O'Connell Street for modern American and English blockbusters.

For live entertainment, we were spoilt for choice as we had three theatres from which to choose – the Abbey in Pearse Street, close to Trinity, the Gaiety in South King Street at the top of Grafton Street and the Gate at the Rotunda at the top of O'Connell Street. Theatre life in Dublin was vibrant, featuring Irish and international plays, the Irish renaissance being championed by Ireland's greatest actor Michael MacLiammoir, who had actually been born English as Alfred Willmore in London.

I came to know him quite well. I first came across him at the Gaiety Theatre in a Victorian melodrama entitled 'East Lynne' from which the famous line 'Gone, and never called me mother' originated. It was high camp and unforgettable.

He was an exceptional man, intelligent, industrious, flamboyant, who immersed himself in Ireland's Celtic culture and language which he wrote and spoke fluently. As a writer, he published a selection of books on the theatre and Ireland, but his most famous theatrical work was his one-man show 'The Importance of being Oscar' about the works of Oscar Wilde which premiered at the Gate in 1960 and went on to be a worldwide success. Most actors have excellent voices but his was deep and well-rounded and immediately recognisable. He was the narrator in the movie 'Tom Jones' in which his exceptional voice complemented the ambience of the movie and, I am sure, helped it towards its four Oscars.

His skill was so good that once he was asked to record the Rubaiyat of Omar Khayyam for the production of a long-playing record. The recording session was set up and he set off on his run through. At the end of the run through, the director said, "That is it. Your run through is perfect. It cannot be improved. We need no more."

This was the Dublin that was basically the centre of our universe for the eight to nine months of our annual scholastic existence. It was now time to get on with organizing our lives.

As we settled into our bed and breakfast dwelling, we were given a bedroom with two single beds with bedside cupboards, the room being lit by a single overhead light. The main furniture comprised a chest of drawers and a large cupboard – the furniture reflecting a genteel past that was having difficulty keeping up. Our sole means of heating was an electric fire which ran off a meter that enthusiastically consumed one shilling pieces (5ps). The bathroom and lavatory were communal.

Our landlady, Mrs Neary, rather resembled her furniture – genteel but old fashioned and not inordinately generous other than with her breakfasts. These covered the whole range of the traditional Irish breakfast including a fried egg, black pudding, bacon, sausage, beans, fried bread, toast and tea.

I am not sure that I went up in her estimation when on the second day that we were staying with her, my new MG Magnette ZB four-seater motor car was delivered to her front door. It was my father's birthday present to me for my recently passed 18th birthday.

It is necessary here, for those who have not yet enjoyed my life story to date, to give a quick resume which may explain my personality and my financial status. I am the only child of parents who were married just before the Second World War and at the end of which, made their life in Hong Kong. My father was a chartered account and neither of my parents came from a wealthy background. They acquired a pleasant life style and moderate wealth by being sensible in their means and by enjoying the advantage of a job well done in a tax-free environment.

One of the results of my strange upbringing, an upbringing that was split between eight years at Catholic boarding schools in England and another life in Hong Kong was that, within reason, I was generously supplied with money. My allowance for my first year at Trinity was £40 per month, equivalent in present money to about £800 per month.

However, in those days the value of the pound was almost twice what its inflation value says it was, as costs were far cheaper. For example, as students, we could play golf on any Irish golf course for 1 shilling and six pence (7.5p) and entry to a racetrack for a shilling (5p).

The same levels of value for money applied in the restaurants, local travel and any rentals that we had to pay. As an example of the difference in the value for money, in Dublin pubs, a pint of Guinness cost 1 shilling and six pence (8p), less outside the centre of town.

My university fees were paid for (approximately £300 per year) and it was at this time that my parents had acquired an apartment at 38 Onslow Square in South Kensington, London, a delightful apartment on the top floor overlooking the Georgian Square which was to be their first retirement and my holiday home.

My first lecture was my chosen subject English and was given by the professor H. O. White. His opening words were to affect my whole career at Trinity. He began by saying, "Most of you here are from an English background and most of you, I assume, can read. May I, therefore, recommend to you that you spend the next four years not just studying but get out and discover the wonder that is Ireland. I do not expect to see you that often in my lectures." This was a recommendation that I took to heart.

My second discovery was rather more problematic. I had forgotten or I had not truly appreciated that the subject of my studies was not English but it was Modern Languages, in the plural. We were expected to study two. On the application form, I must have chosen French as I had staggered through French at O-level. After two French lectures, I realised I was quite out of my depth as their starting standard was A-level. Two languages were taught from scratch – Spanish and

Italian. For obvious reasons, being one quarter Italian, I signed on for Italian, Professor Mr MacMillan.

It was a great choice as fellow students in my class included two wonderful colleagues who later became not only famous as actors but also married – Ralph Bates and Joanna van Gyseghem.

Finally, I was introduced to my tutor, R. B. D. French who enjoyed a delightful, traditional tutor's suite of rooms in the Rubrics, the oldest building in the college which faced across Library Square to the campanile and the front gate. English was his subject but I do not remember that we were required to over-exert ourselves other than the occasional essay to be presented to him. His other and more useful function was to be our mentor if we required moral or administrative advice.

Carl Bontoft (Bon) in reflexive pose

I and my fellow Freshmen/women began to find our way around both within college and outside. Our areas around town were fairly limited on a daily basis and formed a rectangle that at its base was our college, Grafton Street on its right-hand side, St Stephens Green at the top and Kildare Street to the left.

Within this small area were the pubs we frequented such as Davy Byrnes, the restaurants such as the Bailey and, on special occasion days, Jammets, the National Library in Kildare Street (very useful for Italian literature translated into English), Hodges Figgis's bookshop, Bewleys coffee shop,

Fox's tobacconist and Brown Thomas's department store on Grafton Street. There was and perhaps still is an old joke which went what have Grafton Street and an African president got in common? I am sure you have already guessed the answer but it concerns them both having Brown Thomases.

To the side of the chapel was our college library. Other than its fame being us students, it is one of the six British libraries that by law must receive a copy of every book published in the British Isles. It is also home to the majestic Book of Kells, an illuminated manuscript containing the four gospels. It is believed to have been created around 800 AD.

Opposite the chapel in the front square was the Buttery. Here was the dining hall which was used not only for formal occasions when the students and college hierarchy attended in their official gowns but it also supplied daily lunches. A queue, invariably, formed across the square every lunchtime for those wishing to attend.

The only alternative catering establishment within the college grounds was a small café at the junction between three squares, the Rubrics, Botany Bay (home to the only bathhouse) and the most easterly square, quaintly called New Square – though it seemed rather aged to us.

This daily queue at the Buttery gave birth to one of my rather wilder ideas which seemed very amusing at the time if we could have pulled it off. The idea was to embarrass the freshmen who came the year after us.

We would plant within their initial information pack an instruction that they needed to have a urine sample taken at the medical school and to bring it in its glass tube to line up at lunch time in the queue to enter the dining hall.

Others thought that this was a good plan but the logistics defeated us and an embarrassing year for new students never came to pass.

Others, our predecessors by a year, had completed their National Service so were, for the most part, two years older than us, and rather more knowledgeable in the ways of the world. They had the idea of placing a Mini on the roof of the Provost's house which lay behind the chapel and over looked the front square with, behind, the Provost's garden that was walled from the outside of the college.

Through the night, they climbed up on to the roof, assembled wheel and tackle and began to haul up the Mini. Dawn arrived and the car was only half way up. They had to leave it. One of my close friends had been one of the group and explained that they did not know what to do as they were sure that the car would be discovered hanging over the Provost's garden.

If they were to return the following night, would the authorities be lying in wait for them? They decided to finish the job and full of trepidation came back the following night. No one waited for them so they finished the job, disassembled their equipment and went to bed in the early hours delighted with themselves. A delight that was not shared by the authorities but the culprits were never discovered.

This particular friend, when he left college being two years ahead of me, gave me as a parting present a bunch of detonators that he did not know what to do with. They were excellent for stringing along the trees in New Square and setting off to celebrate a birthday or royal occasion. Fortunately, I managed to use them all up before leaving my rooms in college.

The next priority was to decide what extra curricula activities I should undertake. I applied to join the amateur dramatic society known as the 'Players' who had their own theatre in the corner of Front Square. The second one I joined was the rugby club and I thought I might try my hand at sailing yachts. I also presented myself as a possible contributor to the more scurrilous university magazine called TCD, a competitor to the more politically correct Trinity News.

I then joined an unofficial club run by a certain Michael Leehy who held poker nights once a week. I realised very quickly that I could only consider this a charity as I don't think in the brief time I spent in the school that I ever won. I did, however, remain friends with Mr Leehy.

The Players became a part of my university life and generated friendships that were to last most of my life with one in particular, called John Hickmott, with whom I still converse and the Players' musical talent – a man with the wonderful name of Carl Daniel Harald Heinrick Bonaventura Bontoft, Vicompte de St Miuex and de St Quentin, (you couldn't make it up) fortunately reduced to Bon or Bonty. Within the Players were students later to become famous including my classmates Joanna and Ralph but also Mike Bogdanov (then surnamed more simply Bogdin), Terry Brady – both writers and actors and Gay Firth, authoress, known as VAT69 as her maiden name was Gay Virginia Arabella Turtle. Louis Lentin, who directed our plays, became a stalwart of the Irish television and movie networks.

A secondary benefit came as a result of being cast as Creon in a Greek play we presented at the end of my first term. My part only required me entering in the last act. To pass the time, I had set off in the early evening to find a pub relatively close to the theatre.

Just off our usual area of activity on Grafton Street, a street ran right to a pub called the Old Stand. I hadn't realised it at the time but it has been on its present site on Exchequer street for over 300 years. It became one of my regular haunts.

I introduced it to the Players and it became their second home as well. Its great advantage was that not only did it have the friendliest of staff but also it served excellent wild smoked salmon and steaks, very reasonably priced for hungry students.

Players produced an annual serious play towards the end of the winter term but, perhaps more infamously, produced an annual revue at the end of the summer term. The main authors were Mike Bogdin and Terry Brady but contributions came from members of academia as well as a variety of students. Amusing or satirical scripts were interlaced with songs.

We must have had a certain notoriety as members of the revue cast. Many years later, at least 50 to 55, I was at a party in Jamaica with Jamaican friends high up in the Newcastle mountains overlooking Kingston harbour. A couple of their friends asked if they would mind if they brought with them an English lady house guest. On their arrival, I heard my host mention that there was another English guest here, me, and his name was Peter Hunt. She immediately asked did my host know if I had gone to Trinity.

On being introduced, she explained that she had been two years junior to me but had never forgotten the revues and the members of the cast. I have to admit to being rather pleased at her excellent memory and noticed that this had piqued a greater interest in me by my hosts.

Joining the rugby club allowed me to begin to take seriously my English professor's suggestion that we went out and discovered Ireland.

Rugby was taken seriously and I soon discovered that my love of cigarettes, gin and tonic and Guinness meant that I would never qualify for the First team and earn my university 'pink', our sporting equivalent of Oxbridge's 'blue'. I was happy to settle into the second or third team as required.

The opposition that we played would either be against the local police or teams as far away as Belfast in the north, Cork in the south or Limerick and Galway in the west. There were two disadvantages, however. The qualification for joining the Irish Police, known as the Garda Siochana or more commonly Guards, appeared to us to be that you must be at least six feet six inches tall and weigh in at a good 14 stone. You must also be fit. We did not win many games against them but it did mean that you began to know the local police which could be useful at times.

It did not help me initially when I had been drinking at a pub in Westland Row and on leaving, decided I was too drunk to ride my bicycle. As I passed Pearce Street police station, a Guard came out and arrested me for being drunk in charge of a bicycle as I was walking up the middle of the street carrying my bicycle on my shoulder.

One of the college rules was that if you spent the night in a police cell, you may well be rusticated particularly if you came before the Junior Dean or he had been called out to bail you out. Since luck would have it, as I was being charged, a Guard who had been my front row opposition the week before recognised me and I was sent off with a flea in my ear and told to collect my bicycle the following day.

We were convinced that when we went south or west that our opposition fielded two different teams. We would travel to them by coach, arrive to be hosted by the opposing team at a dinner and an evening of drinking and then play our rugby game the following afternoon. The only problem was that we could not recognise, from the previous evening, one person on the opposing playing team but quite a few in the scarce crowd that watched the game – smiling hugely as we suffered yet another defeat.

Rugby front rows have a definite brotherhood and all hostility shown to each other on the field is forgotten in the post-game hospitality. When we played against Queens University in Belfast, it was in the days before 'the troubles'. It surprised me therefore when I was drinking with my opposite number after the game when we started talking about the tension which simmered between Protestant and Catholic.

"Do you know, Peter, I can smell a Catholic at one hundred yards," my opponent exclaimed.

I admit I was rather shocked but replied, "Oh really, what am I?"

"I assume you are a Protestant," he replied.

"No, actually, I am a Catholic."

"Oh, that doesn't count. You're English."

That was the end of that conversation, particularly as Bernadette Devlin did not wake up that particular Irish dragon until some years later.

My interest in yachting was very short lived. I was invited one Saturday to take a sail in a Dragon (a yacht which I knew well) by a member of the prestigious Royal Irish Yacht Club in Dun Laoghaire.

The weather was pretty close to inclement, wind at force five or six and the sea choppy. However, we set off and enjoyed a brisk sail with moments of excitement for an hour or so.

On our return to the marina and as I said my thanks and goodbyes, I was told that the yacht needed to be cleaned. I replied that of course I understood that and that I assumed it was the job for the boat boy. It was then explained to me that I was the boat boy. Not wishing to give offence, I stayed and did what was required but, without my own boat boy, Ah Ling from Hong Kong to do this work for me, I decided to leave yachting to hardier souls than me.

There are, in life, moments that you regret – particularly if your behaviour has been that of a petty criminal.

In our Ballsbridge digs, as I have mentioned, the only electricity supplied by our landlady was the central ceiling light. Everything else electrical was subject to shillings fed into the voracious meter. John and I decided that we would re-wire the system so that all our electrical needs ran from the ceiling light. We created a network of wires falling to the ground where we had the electric fire, a kettle, bedside lights, radio and other small paraphernalia. When we left in the morning, we stored the wires in the cupboard and re-assembled them on our return.

As was bound to happen, one day we forgot. We returned to a furious Mrs Neary, with threats to bring the whole matter to the university authorities and ordered us, once we had made financial reparation, to leave within two days.

We found an apartment by the Irish Sea, in an area called Sandymount, a reasonably short distance from Trinity, driving either through Ballsbridge (salubrious) or through the dock areas of Irishtown and Ringsend (worrying) and I have to admit I could never take the dockland route without making sure that I drove with extra care and greater vigilance.

One day, I had stopped at a red light when a child burst out of a roadside tenement, slammed into the side of the car and fell to the ground. Fortunately, he got up, shook himself and ran back into his home. The light turned green and, given that he seemed to be fine, I travelled on, very glad that I did not have to stop and try to explain what had happened to, perhaps, a hostile crowd. Nothing like imagination running wild to cause that sick feeling that lasts for some time after the event.

The apartment was basic in the extreme. John and I were joined by another of our Downside friends, Michael Church, whose family had been very kind to me when I had nowhere to go on school holidays. They had taken me in and treated me as one of their reasonably large family living in Weybridge.

Our rent was 10 shilling (50p) per week each which gave us one bedroom in which the three of us slept, joined occasionally by a seagull or two who found a way in through the window that we left slightly open to give us some sleeping air. To this was added a sitting/dining room, and bathroom and a wonderful view from our front window over my parked car to the Irish Sea beyond.

The car parked outside attracted the attention of our neighbours, two girls Helen from Belfast and Sheila from Guildford who soon made themselves known to us in the hope of getting a lift to and from college if our times coincided. As they were both very attractive in their own ways, Sheila long-legged, dark haired and good looking, Helen shorter but with a special warmth and beauty in her face and personality, it was no problem to include them in our car share.

John Hickmott whom I had first met in 'Players' (he was the chorus in my first play) became a great friend and he began to show an interest in one of the girls though I was not sure which. He instigated a weekend pilgrimage to a bar, the name of which I can't remember but whose proprietor was named Jack. This bar was towards the top of Grafton Street, opposite the Gaiety Theatre in South King Street, and was approached like an old-time speakeasy down some stairs to the basement. Here, we thought we were terribly sophisticated as we drank pitcher after pitcher of a cocktail called a White Lady (gin, triple sec and egg white). Then, in party mood, walked back down Grafton Street for prawn cocktails in the Bailey.

After one of these sessions, we agreed that the four of us would take a long weekend away from college and travel over to the west of Ireland.

John and I decided that we would toss a coin and whoever won would choose which girl to concentrate on. What the girls may have done to choose us, we never found out. I won and chose Helen. It was the day before we were to set off when John approached me to renegotiate. He explained that he was shorter than me and that Helen was shorter than Sheila so it would make sense that he escorted Helen. I had no reason to disagree, though assumed he preferred Helen anyway. I must have been right, for a year later they were married. I stayed friends with Sheila but, sadly, lost touch with her after we both had left Trinity. The trip was a great success.

It was our first time of travelling west through, first, the centre of Ireland's horse racing studs near Naas, then the agricultural hinterland of the midlands and finally to our chosen first port of call, Killaloe in East County Clare.

We reserved two rooms, one for boys and one for girls, then walked through the village along the River Shannon and planned a boat trip for the following day on Lough Derg, the third largest lake in Ireland.

The weather was delightful, a blessing after the cold weather we had suffered through late September and October. On our second day, rain fell when we were driving along one side of a valley. We stopped and watched in fascination as we sat in sunlight while heavy rain fell on the other side of the valley. Later, when talking to a local, he seemed surprised that we were surprised. To him, this was an everyday event.

Driving was also a delight. Traffic was minimal. I think we saw only a total of five cars on our almost 100 miles across Ireland. The roads did, however, have a peculiarity all their own. You would have a straight road for perhaps 20 miles and at the end of it the most pernicious S bend you could wish for. Then another dead straight 20 miles and another pernicious S bend. It took a little while to get used to this. We assumed that the road designers just became bored with straight lines.

After the next morning boating on the lake, we drove into Limerick to take a tourist whirl around its centre then we returned to Killaloe for the evening. Our trip back to Dublin and to our adjacent homes completed our first grand tour into the heartland of Ireland.

It was now time to concentrate on student life. This usually involved five days of study, one day of sport and one day of leisure, Sunday.

Autumnal and winter Sundays in Dublin, when the town was invariably icy cold, damp and overcast, were short in daylight hours and long in hours that tested our patience. Every shop and means of entertainment were closed.

John, far right, and Helen, second left, at their son's wedding

The saviour of our sanity was the half hour of humour supplied by the BBC in the early Sunday afternoon. This era definitely saw the very best in radio humour. In my parents' day, the favourite was ITMA (It's That Man Again). 'The Goons' ran from 1951 to 1960, 'Beyond our Ken' from 1958 to 1964 and its sequel 'Round the Horne' from 1965 to 1968. But our firm favourite which had to be listened to after every Sunday lunch was the irrepressible and anarchic 'Tony Hancock', first in Hancock's 'Half hour' which started in 1956 and then in his solo show 'Hancock' in 1961.

During these years, Dublin had the strangest drinking laws. Pubs closed at 10 pm. However, if you were a bona fide traveller and travelled five miles outside the centre of Dublin, you found the 'bona fide' pubs, which were open until midnight. This really was an extraordinary concept which we took to with enthusiasm. You drank your fill until 10pm then drove up into the Wicklow Hills to our favourite pub, the Step Inn, in Stepaside to drink even more until you were thrown out at midnight. Then, it was time to tell my car to go home.

The other strange (to us anyway) habit was the Holy Hour. This was the closure of pubs, island wide, for an hour in the afternoon. In most pubs, if you were a regular, there was a snug at the back of the pub in which the landlord would let you rest until the bar opened an hour later. Money could not change hands but if your credit was good, you drank on tick until the bar re-opened. In the deeper country pubs, if your face fitted, you joined the regulars in the snug.

The next problem that needed to be resolved was how to organise a relationship with a girl. People like me, an only son who had been educated in a boys' own school, really had no idea about women despite my first experiences with Valerie in Hong Kong. Obviously, with no brothers and sisters, introductions to girls of my own age were seriously limited.

There was also a general perception by us boys that women were not really interested in sex. They were interested in marriage. We also believed that all women were like our mothers – mothers who appeared to be content to be the home maker, somehow subservient to their husbands. And, in fact, many of our mothers, daughters of the Edwardian Era, did seem to be content with this way of life. I discovered that my mother, for instance, after my father's death, had never paid a bill in her life.

We believed that marriage was the price you paid for a continuous and satisfactory sex life. Weird, eh?

Looking around, it seemed that I was now heading for a period of sexual drought.

Two sisters, Renate and Gita, were students with us and both were extremely good looking but with the added advantage that their mother, Maria, and their step father, Bill, lived in Killiney and understood that students were invariably hungry. There was always a bowl full of hard-boiled eggs by the entrance door of their house and there was always a warm welcome for their children's friends.

Renate, the elder was perhaps softer in nature, Gita the younger perhaps more fiery but it was quite impossible to choose between them so the only option was to be with both or be with one, whilst the other tested out different boyfriends. This happy relationship continued throughout my years in Trinity by the end of which they had both married, one to an Irishman and one to an Englishman – a sensible combination considering their background and education.

A relationship of a different kind was created with one of my English professors, Alec Reid, his wife, Beatrice, and their young son who also lived in Killiney as, oddly enough, did my Italian professor and his family. Alec was a perfect example of the fictional character of the mad professor. His eyesight was appalling and to read, he had to hold a book up to his face. His hair was a wild white tangle and his clothes were invariably in some disarray. He was somewhat portly and weaved rather than walked. He was, however, an authority on the plays of Samuel Beckett and had as a postgraduate, majored in modern English literature.

The tragedy in their lives, however, was that their son was born with a hole in his heart. Once Alec and I had become friendly, he asked if I would do him a great favour. This was to baby sit their son on evenings that they had to attend some function. I expect that the possession of my own motor car may have had some bearing on the request.

The little boy was charming and no problem to look after. In fact, I enjoyed coming out of town and being met in the house's entrance by a table with a 3000-piece jigsaw on it with the notice 'please help make me whole'. Another delight was a table in the kitchen with a well-presented plate of ham or chicken or a pork pie, salad, cheese and fruit.

Very sadly, their son did not live beyond six years old.

Like a holiday, the first term passed in a stately fashion, slowly and with dignity as we found our way around and about, the second and third flew by and it was suddenly time for our end of year exams. Our subjects were divided into two or three parts. In Italian, one part was Italian literature, the other Italian language, where you were tested on translating English into Italian and vice versa. There were three parts to the English examination – language, literature and (I have never understood why) Middle English, from the days of Chaucer.

I had no problems with the English nor with the Italian literature but I knew as I sat the paper on Italian language that I might be in trouble. And it proved to be so. I had never failed an exam before but the results posted on the college notice board confirmed that I had failed Italian. You may well imagine I was distraught. How was I going to explain this to my parents? And, indeed, what was I going to do now?

I assumed that if the worse came to the worst, I could return to Hong Kong and pursue a career there but I had been away from home for a year and felt that it might not be that easy to pick up where I had left off.

My parents were obviously upset but affirmed that if I wanted to stay at Trinity and repeat this first year, they would support me for the next year. If I failed that, their charity might be reconsidered. I decided to stay.

It was time to return to London for the rest of the summer having confirmed to the authorities that I would repeat my year and I was allocated rooms in college for the next two years. My friend, John Tackaberry, with whom I first walked through the gatehouse to Trinity had, much to his surprise, been offered and had accepted a place to study law at Cambridge for the next three years. This left Michael and I to find a third person to share our three bedroomed suite of rooms in Trinity itself for the coming year.

And so, to London for the summer holiday.

Our flat in Onslow Square was on the top floor with a fire escape balcony running along above the garden square. From this balcony, I could climb up onto the flat roof – excellent for sunbathing in the summer. The flat was straightforward in design. The sitting room, dining room and second bedroom (mine) ran along the side of the square, the master bedroom (my parents), a bathroom, a cupboard, second bathroom and kitchen ran along the south side. There was an extra storeroom in the basement and a caretaker, Mr Jones, who managed buildings 38 and 36. In all the years that I lived there, I always called him Mr Jones, he always called me Peter – as a good employee should, I suppose!

Beneath our flat lived a famous left-handed golfer, fighter pilot and member of parliament, Percy (Laddie) Lucas. His brother-in-law was Douglas Bader, another fighter pilot who had lost both legs in an accident just before the Second World War but he continued to fly and became a prisoner of war.

The film 'Reach for the Sky' documents this part of his career. He was very determined, rather short tempered and outspoken. We sometimes shared the lift.

I hadn't realised that we were both members of the same golf club, the Berkshire, near Ascot.

One Sunday, I was picked to play with him. On meeting him, I asked if he took a buggy. Pipe clenched in his teeth, he first looked at me as if I had just climbed out from under a stone, took his pipe from his mouth, stood squarely in front of me and said, "What do you think I am – a damned cripple that can't walk the course like everyone else?" I stammered an apology and I don't think I hit a decent shot for the rest of the morning. I remember that he won quite easily.

From a painting of Onslow Square towards our apartment

Onslow Square has an interesting history. It was created by the Henry Smith Charity. A certain Henry Smith who was an alderman, landowner and money lender in the City of London created the charity in his will of 1628. In 1685, the charity established an estate by purchasing tracts of farmland to the west of London in areas knows as Kensington and Chelsea.

Nearly 200 years later, in 1845, a Charles James Freake approached the trust with a plan to develop the farmland into a square with a church at one end and houses around the central garden square. George Basavi was appointed the architect; the plans were approved and the square including St Paul's Church was completed in 1865.

In 1995, the trust sold the estate for £280 million.

The London of my teenage years and early twenties was spent mainly within a rectangle with occasional forays outside of it. The southern arm was the River Thames from Putney in the west to the city in the east.

The eastern arm ran up to Oxford Street and west to Notting Hill Gate.

The western arm ran from Notting Hill Gate back down to the river.

London was further sub-divided by those who lived south of the river, those who lived between the river and Hyde Park and those who lived north of Hyde Park. My friends and I lived mainly in the in-between areas of Mayfair, Knightsbridge, Kensington, Earls Court, Chelsea and Fulham – to some known as the world of the Sloane Rangers: a group of privately educated young ladies from privileged backgrounds who lived or fraternised with those who did live in Mayfair or Chelsea.

These areas were like small villages and each sub-division had them. In the north, amongst others, there was Golders Green and Hampstead, to the north of the city, Islington and out to the West Barnes, Wimbledon and Mortlake. Each village had its own character seen either in its architecture or style of clothing or general political thought and practices.

You may have noticed that I have given no examples of the villages south of the river. It might be disgraceful to admit it but we didn't have any reason to go there other than to drive through on our way to the south coast.

The east end was known as the home of the Cockneys with their pearly king and queen and their rhyming slang language but more seriously for the criminal fraternities and assorted villains who in the mid to late 1950s had taken over or opened a succession of gambling cum escort clubs, clubs such as the '21' and 'Churchills' to name just two.

It was also home to a famous pub, 'The Prospect of Whitby' in Wapping; the pub claiming to be the oldest riverside pub in London dating back to 1520. It was very popular with those of us who lived further west as an oasis on a Sunday morning particularly as you were offered, in order to wash down more beer, handfuls of brown shrimps.

Chinese restaurants had been established for years in London but it was in the 1950s and 1960s that streets in Soho became the London Chinatown whereas before the War and the destruction by the Germans of the East End it had been in the Limehouse area. To us, however, we would often travel out of an evening to the East End to visit three Chinese restaurants called the Good, the Old and the New Friends which we considered to be more authentic than the newer ones in Soho.

The major changes occurring during the 1950s, but almost imperceptibly, were three-fold. The first came from the positive economic boom driving out the depression of the aftermath of the devastating war. The second was the emergence of my age group who were questioning the strictness of family and social behaviour, called rather oddly

Victorian, that had been accepted by certainly the middle class of our parents' generation. The third was the beginning of the social mobility of people of talent from the north and the midlands, creating a new excitement in London particularly in the arts, in music and in fashion.

Arriving back in London, after more than a year's absence, I suddenly found that I was on my own. One of my two John friends (Tackaberry) was now deeply involved in his life of study in Cambridge and the other John (Burns) had, through family contacts, become employed as a stockbroker. I must say this surprised me. He was a charming young man but his knowledge of mathematics was decidedly limited as was his general common sense. In fact, these two limitations were to cause a personal disaster. He explained to me one day that in the stock market you could purchase on credit stocks and shares at the beginning of the month but only have to pay for them at the end of the month. If they went up, you received a cheque. If they went down, you paid up.

Through the late '50s and early '60s the market kept going up so John was investing more and more. However, in 1962, the market crashed by 20% and John lost so much that he could not settle. He had to turn to his parents for help. They managed to settle his bills for him but at great cost to their own comfort and to John's peace of mind. I learnt a very salutary lesson from his misfortune and, though I have had investments in the stock market, I also made sure that they were invested in low-risk shares and I never really dabbled.

Somehow, this holiday passed. My major occupations were going to the cinema or walking around Hyde Park or visiting museums or Harrods. To be honest, I was rather at a loss and glad to be heading back to Dublin to start my second year. I felt I couldn't put down any roots in London like trying to join a rugby club or creating any special friendships, (actually with whom as I did not know anyone), as I was to spend the next four years in Dublin.

So, into the car and up to Liverpool via the now defunct Runcorn Conveyor, a wonderful mobile platform that conveyed vehicles across the Mersey, and on to Liverpool and the ferry for Dun Laoghaire.

It is hard to believe now but driving was a pleasure in the late 1950s and 1960s. The population was approximately 50 million in 1960 of which 80% did not own a car. By 2020, the population had exploded to 70 million with 80% owning cars. It is no wonder that driving now can be a stressful and frustrating occupation.

On board, I bumped into Deidre, one of my colleagues at university so we settled down for a couple of drinks at the bar and then into dinner.

After dinner, we went out on deck to watch the lights of the harbour recede behind us and as I looked forward, I said to her that I was sure that a vessel coming towards us looked as if it was on a collision course with us.

The boat came closer and closer and we moved back down our side of the ferry just as the two boats collided, the one entering damaging the port side of our ferry and staving in some cabins on that side – fortunately, not harming anyone though giving some passengers in their cabins a rude shock. We limped back into Liverpool and the next day we were flown to Dublin, my car being delivered over to Dun Laoghaire a few days later.

An experience that I, fortunately, have not had repeated so far in my life as it was decidedly frightening because at the moment of collision, all the sprinklers on our ferry burst open making us believe that we were sinking. It was the only time that I remember Deidre giving me an enormous hug as we thought we might be going down.

I arrived back at college to find that I had been allocated rooms on the top floor of house 37 on the corner of New Square. Between houses 37 and 39 was a gap for cars to pass through on their way to the sports fields and the medical school. Michael Church and I were to be joined by our third member, someone I did not know well but he was an extraordinary character, flamboyant in the extreme who made no pretension of not being gay or queer as homosexuals were called in those days. He was the musical expert from Players – Carl Daniel Harald Heinrich Bonaventura Bontoft, Vicompte de St Mieux and de St Quentin, known commonly as Bon or Bonty.

Bon was given the room overlooking Pearse Street whilst Michael and I had the two overlooking the square. Next to Bon's room was an area that held a sink and a gas cooker. The only other room was our sitting room which included a coal fire, our only means of heating and into which soon arrived an upright piano. The lavatory was communal and was at the back of the entrance to the building on the ground floor, an entrance that had no doors and so was open to all weathers.

I wonder what today's students would have thought of it. It certainly had history but little else. What it did have, however, was our servant known as a Skip. Ours was a Mr Fitzpatrick whom we suspected of conveying fleas into our rooms as we had constantly to powder our beds with DDT. However, he was jolly and he did make our beds, bring up hot water in the morning and coal for our fire as well as doing the small amount of washing up and making an effort to keep our rooms reasonably clean and under control.

It did not take us long to work out a system of cooking. We purchased a large saucepan and it was the duty of each of us in turn to keep the saucepan ready for the next day. It was our choice what we added to the residue. Sometimes a tin of beans or stewing steak or tomatoes would be added, anything that one thought might be interesting to add new flavours to the mix before it was re-heated each day. This made for interesting eating though we limited its continuance to a week at a time, as it could end up virtually inedible.

We were eligible for two baths a week. These were taken in the college's bathhouse, in another square called Botany Bay, which also had showers and more lavatories as well as tennis courts. It has to be admitted that college living was pretty basic but it is surprising how soon you became used to it. In fact, we thought we were privileged to be living in college, close to everything that we might require with no commuting. I even had free car parking for my car through the Lincoln Inn's entrance by the medical school.

It was early in this term that I became friendly with Neville. He had been a member of the party responsible for placing a Mini on the roof of the Provost's house. He had a quirky humour and a dash of devilment in his character. He would have been two years my senior but, somehow, we took to each other at almost our first meeting. Through him, I was to discover a completely different side to Dublin life because he was married to Peggy, a delightful and lively Dublin girl whose family lived in Glasnevin in the northern reaches of the city. Later, I was to be godfather to their daughter.

Glasnevin was very much a newly developed area of north Dublin but, because the airport further north was developing rapidly, so was Glasnevin.

The area itself represented a post-war development with streets of modern detached houses along tree-lined streets in contrast to the tenements and slums that were still very evident further in towards the River Liffey. It was not until the mid-1960s that the city began to clear the slum areas and not again until the boom of the 1970s, Ireland having joined the EU in 1973 that the city became unrecognisable through a programme of mass commercial development.

Despite this, Peggy's family, the Coonaghs, maintained all the traditional facets of a middle-class Catholic family that had an inbred concept of hospitality and good manners. They also spoke with the sing song Irish lilt, slightly nasal, which is very much a feature of born and bred Dubliners.

Peggy was the eldest of seven, five sisters and one brother, youngsters who were delightful company when we were, as happened quite often, invited by their parents to join them for a Sunday lunch out at their golf club to the west of the city. The great advantage of this was that virtually everything was shut on a Sunday but at private clubs you could enjoy liquor with your meal. It was often a merry party that returned to Dublin after lunch for tea at their home.

At much the same time, Dublin saw a dramatic development in its traditional method of shopping as the supermarkets began their irreversible change to the way we shop. A serious contender that eventually saw out much of the competition during the 1960s was the firm of Dunne, originally from Cork. By the end of the 1960s, the Dunne stores numbered 17 across Ireland and they were the first in

1966 to open an out-of-town shopping centre near Dun Laoghaire called Cornelscourt.

Many thought at the time that it would not be a success but they were proved spectacularly wrong. It is still going strong.

It was strange for me to settle into a second year as a repeat of my first year. I knew I had to come to an accommodation somehow as it would be ridiculous for me to repeat my study of English in which I had been successful as I had also been in Italian literature. The major problem had been my grasp, or lack of it, in the complications of the Italian language.

I approached my tutor R. B. D. French and we did come to a strange accommodation. I would be a first-year student in Italian both in language and literature but I would be a second-year student in English.

This arrangement was to stand me in good stead in my fifth year as I was able to add an extra year of reading in both languages.

With this arrangement in place, my second year began and it was surprisingly easy to slip back into all that I had achieved or at least enjoyed in my first year. All my friends were the same with the added advantage of some new faces in the Italian classes – faces that treated me as a fount of all knowledge for life in college and in Dublin.

I also became editor of our more scurrilous magazine TCD in which I wrote whole page articles about people whom I felt should be humorously criticised. This gave rise to a play on my name that I wish I had thought of myself. My competing magazine 'Trinity News' took exception to an article I wrote and so had a go at me. My full name is John

Peter Vernon Hunt so they entitled their article 'The shame of Vermin Grunt'. Glorious!

As a threesome, we soon settled in to life in our rooms. One of our more amusing entertainments, we thought, was to wait for cars passing beneath through the gap between ours and the next building and drop contraceptives full of water on to their windscreen. Well, we thought it funny!

Another, though rather useful, addition to our lives was a rope that we strung up between our room and the rooms adjacent. We tied a basket to it so if in need of sugar, milk, tea or whatever we would shout across and we could exchange supplies as needed.

In the adjacent rooms, one of the three living there was a young man called Jonah. He was athletic, very good looking and seemed to be the only one of us who had a regular girlfriend.

What he was not was academic, so at the end of his second year, he was asked to leave college. Not knowing what to do with himself, he returned home to Cornwall and began to play squash seriously. His full name is Jonah Barrington and he became world squash champion six times between 1967 and 1973.

Bon proved to be a great addition to our living arrangements particularly as he had a universal knowledge of music from classical to popular and would often, on a wet and miserable evening, play his piano and sing songs from Carmina Burana or by Noel Coward.

Neville must have been bored one afternoon so he attached a tin tack to each of the hammers of Bon's upright. I assumed that Bon would be furious but he roared with laughter when he first played his new harpsichord and it was quite some time before he returned his piano to its original state.

It was towards the end of my second year that I was to meet a couple who changed my life at university. I had decided to have a party in our rooms and went off into town to find a wine merchant. I entered one in Kildare Street to be greeted by an assistant, an English man named Peter Powrie.

We took an immediate liking to each other and, after we had met a few times, he explained that he was going to start a restaurant and had his eye on a small restaurant called the Soup Bowl in Molesworth Lane, a street between Grafton and Kildare streets, very much in the heart of our Dublin.

He was successful in purchasing it and he and his Irish wife Kathie began to create the restaurant of their dreams first by continuing to serve lunches and dinners but with the idea as it became more financially secure to turn it into a more select and specialised restaurant.

It was not large. The downstairs eating area held perhaps five to six tables allowing a maximum of 30 people while upstairs there was a larger room which could hold perhaps the same number but in more comfort. Behind the ground floor eating area was the kitchen and below in the basement the wine cellar and in its very early days where they slept. There was a small yard out back for a lavatory and waste bins. It was compact and manageable.

Peter was the chef, Kathie ran the front of house and it was not long before I was helping out sometimes washing up, sometime waiting on tables even helping Peter cook.

My cooking was obviously up to scratch as one morning I answered the telephone to find that Peter and Kathy had been partying up country and had overslept. Would I, could I do the lunches? I remember that the favourite lunchtime dish was Boeuf Bourguignon. Whilst preparing it, I went into the cellar to find a suitable bottle of wine. They all looked much the same to me so I took the first one to hand. It was only later that Peter told me that I had taken one of the most expensive reds. There were certainly no complaints from the customers that day.

Our friendships blossomed as the restaurant became more successful and Peter and Kathie soon found themselves an apartment in Ballsbridge.

I think that it was at the start of my third year that they changed the restaurant completely. They stopped doing lunches and concentrated on the downstairs restaurant leaving the upstairs empty except for special functions. The restaurant was only lit by candles and this created an intimate atmosphere quite unlike anything else in Dublin.

In a very short time, it became a favourite evening haunt of people from the media and the arts as well as the nouveau rich that were becoming a feature of Dublin life.

The dinner menu was limited, specialising in steaks, duck and salmon in the style of a sophisticated bistro. It was strange to think that on one of my trips back from London that I introduced them to avocadoes, a novelty at the start of the 1960s.

This success began to attract actors and actresses who were filming in Ardmore studios just outside Dublin. Being filmed was a re-make of Somerset Maugham's novel 'Of Human Bondage', the story of a medical student played by Lawrence Harvey who falls in love with a waitress played by Kim Novak. An appeal had gone out for extras and I had applied and had been accepted to play (be) a fellow medical student. I think we were paid about £4.00 per day with a £1 an hour for overtime – infrequent but a wonderful bonus when we ran into overtime.

Being an extra is tedious to say the least. Having a short four-letter surname which can be the butt of mispronunciation can also be a bonus. There were about 40 of us extras, all in period costume and required to be dressed by 8am. The costume suppliers seemed to have no difficulty remembering my name so I was called up first, dressed and off for tea and a bacon sandwich (freely supplied) to await the day's action. Whenever that may be!

I excelled with my one starring role. I had to walk behind Lawrence Harvey and Brian Forbes who were chatting and hang up my white medical coat on a coat hanger on the wall. I walked in from the right, hung up my coat to stand appalled as the hanger and my coat fell with a crash to the floor. The two stars burst out laughing which did not help my embarrassment as the scenery people repaired the hanger. If you don't blink, you see my performance in the finished movie.

My only other moment before the camera was to sit at a table in a café while Kim Novak waited on Lawrence Harvey at the next table. She was a very beautiful woman but, sadly, paid no attention to the adoring extra at the next table.

One evening, Lawrence Harvey and his partner Mrs Cohn, the widow of Harry Cohn of Columbia Pictures, came in to the Soup Bowl for dinner. She was wearing so many diamonds that we thought the electric light had been turned on – a very striking couple.

A couple of nights later, Lawrence Harvey was at one table, Peter O'Toole at another, Peter Finch at another and

Siobhan McKenna at a fourth. Through the early evening, they all behaved as if the others were not in the room. They were little pools of isolation but then the wine flowed and the evening ended up with the four of them singing and dancing on the tables of the restaurant much to the distress of management who could see their tables being destroyed for ever. They were not and the amount of the bill was a most satisfactory consolation.

Film stars, or the very few that I have met, do have a magnetic personality. One evening Lawrence Harvey gave a dinner party in the upstairs room at the Soup Bowl for his crew at the end of filming. I was the waiter for the evening. The crew arrived and went upstairs and I noticed that though pleasant enough there was not a lot of life to the party. The minute Harvey walked in it was if a light had been switched on, the party livened up and eventually became hilarious.

At the end of the evening as they were leaving, Harvey's stand-in came up to me and offered me a £10 note. I explained that I was a student and not a professional waiter and I couldn't accept a tip. He looked at me as if I came from Mars and whispered in my ear, "He won't miss it. He wants you to have it and you deserve it. So, take it and spend it unwisely." I must admit I swallowed my pride and took it.

It has to be remembered that homosexuality was illegal in those days though, through Bon, I met members of a vibrant homosexual society in Dublin which seemed to have two distinct social classes. There was the middle class of media, theatrical and business men and there was what they described as 'rough trade', men from the docks and the tenement areas.

I had returned from London one night and was in the Soup Bowl but had no accommodation arranged until the following day. I was expecting to sleep in the basement of the restaurant. One of the customers, Alphie, a senior designer in Irish Television, a well-known homosexual, offered to give me a bed for the night knowing and on the understanding that I was not queer.

I accepted and we went to sleep in his bedroom in two separate single beds. Just before falling asleep, Alphie began to chat me up with a chat line that I practiced later for my own use. It was based on the premise that if you haven't tried something you don't know whether you would like it or not. I can assure you that the siren's call did not go unnoticed but it did not get me to hop into his bed just to find out.

I have mentioned that one of our favourite late-night pubs was the Step Inn in Stepaside. Sometimes, when I arrived there, I found that Bon was already there with one of his 'rough trade' friends and he asked me if I could give them a lift back into college. If I liked his friend, I would say there was room in the car. If not, that he would have to go in the boot. Stepaside was a good seven miles back to college down winding mountain roads. The condition of the poor boy who had come back in the boot of the car would not be in a fit state for great love making I would have thought.

My second year had come to an end and I was now 20 and looking to create some sort of life in London for the holidays when I was there.

Great friends of mine from Hong Kong Betty and Everard were on long leave in London and some years before Betty had said that if I ever met her elder daughter Annabel there would be trouble. I had met her daughter as a thirteen-year-old one summer in Hong Kong and thought her very pretty but took no further interest in her as she was a girl far too young for me.

I now met her in London and she was stunning. We began to secretly see each other, meeting for coffees and looking delightfully into each other's eyes. Betty found out and threatened to take a shot gun to me if I continued to see her daughter. This, of course, intensified our desire to see each other.

Annabel was taking classes in a language school and I had arranged to meet her there to take her out for lunch. Her language teacher was called John Perridge and he obviously found her very attractive as well as he too wanted to take her out to lunch. The three of us went together and John realising that I was top of the batting order agreed to be our conduit for making assignations.

John was to become a lifelong friend and a major London companion. He had suffered from rickets as a child so did not reach a great height but this seemed to make him more determined to succeed and to enter, enthusiastically, with getting on with his life. He was also a brilliant linguist being fluent in four languages and interested in others. As an example, one year we were in Spain on the beach and he, I and another friend were in a six-division beach shower with a German girl and a Spanish girl in adjacent showers that we wanted to chat up. John spoke to each of the girls in their own language whilst translating from ours without a pause or a second thought.

We were very impressed as I did get a date with the German girl whom I remember as attractive but not very adventurous. It was certainly no holiday romance.

This was a time when there could be, regrettably quite often, flare ups and punch ups between English and German youths particularly in holiday resorts. I can only hope that my brief relationship with one of Germany's young ladies gave at least one example of English good manners if not much else.

This particular trip to Spain where John owned an apartment was with me, his new girlfriend, an Australian called Kerrie, who was soon to become his wife and her visiting sister, Susan. John was a great admirer of bullfighting and managed to talk his way into the barrier area between the ring and the audience where the performers in this death ritual were positioned whilst the matador did his stuff out in the arena.

The matador is the master of the ring and it is his responsibility not only to torment and kill the bull but also to oversee all that happens in the ring. This particular day, the matador was Curro Romero, considered one of Spain's better matadors though not considered by the cognoscenti to be the most courageous. The bull was reared by the Domecq family, famous for their sherry as well as for raising a stable of fighting bulls.

No one quite knows how it happened but John was taking photographs in the barrier when the bull escaped Romero's attentions and jumped over the barrier. John could not run and received a goring from the bull which resulted in one of his horns piercing through John's upper thigh. The wound can be fatal and is known in bullfighting parlance as a 'herida fatal'. John was taken off to hospital and became something of a local celebrity for surviving the wound. The one criticised was not John but Romero for not controlling the arena.

Soon after his recovery, he received an invitation from the Domecq hierarchy in Jerez as a salute to his bravery to come over to visit their vineyards and winery by having lunch with them and then spending a night in a Jerez hotel at their expense. John explained that there were four of us and the invitation was extended gracefully to us all.

John's car was a Triumph TR4 sports car so the roof was down and he and I sat in the front with the girls in the back. The journey to their hacienda took just over two hours and we were suitably dust laden and sweaty when we arrived to be met by father and son Domecq, most beautifully dressed in their finest suits, ties and shirts. We really wished that the trip would have been the other way around and we could have gone to the hotel first to change before meeting them for lunch.

However, our hosts' manners were impeccable and we were given a wonderful lunch, sampling various different sherries first, and then, a tour of the vineyards – a splendid afternoon followed by a delightful evening in Jerez as guests of the members of the Domecq family.

My relationship with Annabel continued to blossom, meeting whenever we could for lunch or coffee, made more exciting by the fact that her mother had banned me from seeing her and we both enjoyed the secretive arrangements for meeting each other. This enjoyable but innocent embryonic love affair continued until I had to return to Dublin. We continued to communicate through letters sent to our mutual friend, John, at her school.

John and Kerrie Perridge

On returning to London, Annabel's mother's attitude changed and I was welcomed as her daughter's accepted boyfriend and, thereafter, spent time with her family. This made life much simpler and Annabel's 16th birthday was three days before my 21st, which we celebrated with my parents at the Savoy hotel, cabaret by Jimmy Edwards, then one of England's famous comedians.

My present from my parents for my 21st birthday took me completely by surprise. My father gave me a cheque for £21,000. The agreement was that I would not spend the capital but would enjoy the income. My father, on his deathbed, assumed that I had blown the capital a long time ago. I was able to assure him that I could give him a cheque for the £21,000 there and then. He smiled, I think, with satisfaction.

I did, however, lose quite a lot of it later on trying to promote baseball in England but that was in the future.

Later that year, our relationship ground to a halt as Annabel and her parents returned to Hong Kong and I returned to Dublin. I was not sure that I would ever see her again.

Being very involved with a girlfriend who isn't there affects any intention you might have of pursuing other girls. There were more choices now with that year's influx but I found it difficult to raise any enthusiasm.

To console me, John and Helen invited me to meet her sister, Katherine, and her husband, Laine, who lived in Coleraine in Northern Ireland and to spend a long weekend with them. My previous ventures to the north had only been to Queens University in Belfast so I had never been out into the countryside.

On route, it was an opportunity to visit the city of Armagh, the town in which St Patrick, Ireland's patron saint, founded his main church with surrounding convents and monasteries at some time in the fifth century.

It is a city that has the distinction of being the ecclesiastical capital of Ireland – seat to the primates of all Ireland for both the Roman Catholic Church and the Protestant Church of Ireland. Because of this, it has two cathedrals, one for each form of Christianity, and both of them dedicated to St Patrick.

Sadly, however, despite its religious egalitarianism, during the 'Troubles', various atrocities happened there and 86 people were killed in the city.

Parts of Northern Ireland are really beautiful from the Mountains of Mourne in the south to the Giant's Causeway in the north but much of the county is lush countryside, perfect for breeding horses and cattle and for agriculture.

The border between Northern Ireland and Eire runs almost from west to east, over 300 miles of rugged countryside with close to 300 public roads intersecting it. It is virtually impossible to police and the difference in prices and taxes between the British and Irish economies allowed a serious amount of smuggling between both sides of the border.

Later, friends in the town of Ballyjamesduff, a town reasonably close to the border, explained that most of the wealthy houses in the area were the result of some successful inter-border transactions!

However, our interest during the weekend other than enjoying true Northern Irish hospitality was to hack our way round the championship golf course at Port Stewart and to enjoy its adjoining rugged northern coastline which included a trip to the Giant's Causeway situated near the town of Bushmills, famous for its production of Bushmills Whiskey. Obviously, a pub stop and a sampling of its famous product were obligatory.

Annabel and me at my 21st

Returning to Dublin, I immersed myself back into college life, to working in the Soup Bowl and continuing to study. The good news came by airmail letter. Annabel was returning to Europe to take up a French course in Paris. Would I like to travel over to see her? I have to admit a little pitter patter of my heart oddly intermingled with trepidation as to how it would be when we saw each other again. It might be a possible disaster and the return trip from Paris to Dublin, a miserable one. Nothing like being optimistic!

By good fortune, Air Lingus were taking a new Boeing 720 jet aircraft over to Paris for an inaugural flight somewhere and I, somehow, managed to thumb a lift. It was good fun being the only passenger on board with a full cabin crew and being jokingly threatened by the pilots that they might do a barrel roll aerobatic manoeuvre to see if the aircraft was strong enough to take it or whether the wings would fall off and the fuselage descend rather quickly into the Irish Sea.

They didn't and, joy of joys, Annabel was there to meet me at the airport and looking as beautiful as ever.

Our reunion was ecstatic and we commiserated all the time on how we had been away from each other for far too long. We spent a delightful long weekend being young lovers in Paris and visiting Versailles and Fontainebleau as well as sharing baguettes and bottles of wine in wayside cafés – almost living by a film script of the young in Paris. It always amused me that if Annabel happened to be sitting at a café on her own waiting for me and was approached by a Parisian hoping to pick her up. Her reply was always, "J'attends mon fiancé. Il est un boxeur." It seemed to work remarkably well as a deterrent.

A further result of our reunion was an invitation by Annabel's parents to join them on a holiday in Greece. Obviously, I was now an accepted appendage to their family arrangements.

The family had rented a villa in Vouliagmeni near Athens so this was a chance to discover the city and to be amazed by its history and architecture. Rome, of course, I knew well as my father's mother lived there but I had not realised how spectacular the ancient Greek monuments are in Athens, in particular the Parthenon that dominates the city.

I would hate to think that the most memorable thing about Athens was the glass of citron pressé served by a vendor at the walk up to the Parthenon but it was seriously delicious.

For a long weekend, we left Vouliagmeni and travelled to look at the Corinth Canal then on to Delphi on the slopes of Mount Parnassus where we booked into a local hotel. After dinner, Annabel and I went for a walk down the road towards the ruins. It was a full moon and as we rounded a corner, we came across the ruins of the temple of Athena Pronaia bathed in bright, bright moonlight. It was stunning and magical. The atmosphere was so unique that you could imagine the oracle preparing for a visitation from some famous Greek hero to find out his future. It was a special moment in my life and one I have never forgotten.

We would now see each other with far greater frequency including Annabel coming over for a holiday with me in Ireland. After a few days introducing her to Trinity and Dublin, we headed south through Wicklow, Waterford and Cork. Here, we made a detour to Blarney to take the opportunity to kiss the Blarney stone and achieve 'the gift of the gab'.

In order to kiss the stone which is set in the wall below the battlements, you climb to the castle's peak and, at an opening in the wall, you lie on your back and lower your head over the edge of the wall to kiss the stone on the wall facing you. Below you is open space, though now there are guardrails to stop you falling. It is quite scary but exhilarating. Annabel was not fully prepared as she was wearing a mini-skirt and realised that much would be on view as she lay on her back her head over the wall.

She greatly appreciated that the attendant, obviously used to this problem, offered a rug to cover her legs so saving her blushes and dignity.

We continued through to Killarney where we stayed to admire the famous lakes and the wonderfully named mountains that mark the eastern end of the Ring of Kerry, the MacGillycuddy's Reeks. Driving round the Ring is one of the great tourist attractions in Ireland and deservedly so for the scenery is outstanding both along the coast and inland around the Reeks themselves.

It was now time for us to undertake the 300-mile journey back to Dublin and for me to wave farewell to Annabel at the airport as she flew back home. I would see her at the end of term back in London. Something to look forward to.

The summer term came to an end and with it the examinations to decide my future. To be honest, I still did not like the look of the Italian language paper but, somehow, I staggered through it and, joy of joys, when the results were posted I had passed and was set on course for another three years in Trinity.

I packed my bags, loaded the car and set off for a summer in England with Annabel and her family.

History has painted the 1960s as the age of counterculture and seems to concentrate on personalities in the fashion, music and media worlds. However, this decade, the so-called decade of the 1960s really only began half-way through the 1960s with the birth of the Beatles in 1962, sophisticated London clubs such as 'Annabel's' in 1963, 'Tramps' in 1969 and elegant restaurants like the 'White Elephant' in 1961. (There were many more but I was fortunate enough to be a member of three of these and a friend of Leslie Linder, the owner of the 'White Elephant').

John Aspinall, who had been instrumental in 1960 in having the gaming laws relaxed, led the way for many gaming clubs including his own flagship the Clermont in Berkeley Square and, later, the introduction of the Playboy Club to London's West End.

One of the oldest private members' gaming clubs, 'Les Ambassadeurs' (more commonly known as Les A) in 1950 moved to its famous premises at five Hamilton Place in Mayfair. The Garrison nightclub was opened in the basement in the early 1960s and became a personal favourite.

Jean Shrimpton, Mary Quant's miniskirts, the King's Road, Carnaby Street, youth and the West End of London became the marker posts of the idea of Swinging London. In 1961, the birth control pill was introduced, though initially only for married women. In 1967, it was finally made available to all women. It is considered to be one of the most important factors in the change of sexual freedom which began in this decade.

However, the reality was somewhat different.

In 1960 a new voice of socialism, Harold Wilson, had given the public his speech on the 'white heat of this scientific revolution' and his party won the election in 1964 bringing in socialism to a society tired of successive Conservative governments since the war. In part, this was responsible for far more involvement by left wing union activity culminating in an unofficial strike by the miners that caused havoc and lasted two weeks. It was a forerunner of strike after strike led by the miners in the next decade.

1961 was to feature two dramatic events which seriously threatened the peace of the West. The first, in April, was an attempt by Cuban exiles to oust Castro by invading Cuba. They were aided and abetted by the Americans but their attacking forces were defeated by Castro at the Bay of Pigs.

The relationship between Russia and the West continued to harden not only with the creation of the Berlin Wall but also Russia went to support Castro by placing intercontinental ballistic missiles designed to carry atomic bombs on the island facing America. As young twenty-year olds, we seriously believed, as the crisis worsened in 1962, that the Third World War might be declared and we would be called up to fight against Russia at the side of our recent American allies. Somehow, and you will understand our enormous relief, the two presidents, Kennedy and Khrushchev came to an understanding and the missiles were withdrawn.

The 1960s were no stranger to war and assassinations that shocked the world and kept the thought in our minds of conscription into the armed forces.

From 1955, the Americans had continuously increased their involvement in Vietnam and, in 1964, 184,000 combat troops were sent to join the fighting. In 1965, the Indo-Pakistan war broke out; in 1967, the six-day war between Israel and Egypt and her allies began and, in 1968, the student riots in Paris caused enormous disruption. In 1963, President Kennedy was assassinated and in 1968 both his brother Robert Kennedy and Martin Luther King Jr were also assassinated. As well as all of this, there were various sections of society that included feminism, gay pride, black power, anti-Vietnam demonstrations and hippies demanding attention.

For us locally, in 1964, the new labour government under Harold Wilson brought in exchange controls whereby we were only allowed to purchase £50 per year in foreign currency. As you can imagine, this was widely flouted but it still limited to a large extent any foreign travel.

For many, however, one of the benefits of the 1960s was in the world of travel.

In 1966, Freddy Laker created Laker Airways, a novel idea for a low cost/no frills airline that became Skytrain in 1977. Though the airline went bust in 1982, it was the business model for the present-day cut-price airlines such as Virgin, Easy Jet, Norwegian Air and Ryanair amongst others. Having first been involved in package holidays, Freddy Laker may well be considered the father of the boom in holiday travel which continues to this day.

Another revolution that the 1960s heralded was the proliferation of television stations competing with the BBC and the introduction of colour television in 1967. Television allowed the creation of a new style of humour initiated to a great degree by four university graduates, Peter Cook, Dudley Moore, Alan Bennett and Jonathan Miller in their ground breaking satirical show 'Beyond the Fringe'. This led to other shows such as 'That was the week that was', and eventually the 'Monty Python' series.

The moral standards of good manners and the acceptance of law and order, the church, the military, politics and the legal profession were seen as valid targets for satire.

Late night cabarets had always been popular in the private clubs but with the fascinating figure of Danny La Rue who opened his own late-night club in Hanover Square, the concept of drag queens became accepted. Even more important for the homosexual fraternity, homosexuality between consenting adults was legalised in 1967.

London and the other major conurbations were enjoying a freedom that our parents would have considered shocking and the voice of Mary Whitehouse was constantly challenging what she termed a total breakdown in decency and morality. It became an important but a lone voice out in the wilderness.

During my third year, Alex and Beatrice Reid whose son had now died, invited Annabel and me to their holiday home on the island of Cephalonia in Greece. We decided to make a full holiday of it and trained down to the tip of Italy and in the footsteps of Gerald Durrell (author of 'My family and other animals') took the ferry across to Corfu.

I have not been back to Corfu but in the 1960s it was a delightful island, a mixture of ancient temples, romantic palaces and quiet, unspoilt beaches and villages. Hillsides were tree-covered in olives and cypresses, goats wandered fearlessly onto and across roads, the Ionian Sea, a deep blue that sparkled both in sunlight and moonlight and the local populace, though neither of us understanding a word of each other's language, communicated happily by smile and gesture.

We hired a small motor bicycle and spent an almost hedonist week visiting sites or lazing on a beach and eating lobsters washed down by local wines, keeping the rather strong Retsina wine for evenings as an excess of it could produce a violent hangover.

After a week, we took a ferry from Corfu south to Cephalonia, an island that had been devastated by earthquakes in 1953. Virtually every house in the south of the island had been destroyed and many in the north but recovery was evident and the olive trees, approximately a million of them, seemed to have survived and were a major source of income to the farmers on the island.

Fiskardo, a village and small harbour on the northern tip of Cephalonia where our hosts had their holiday home, was fortunate in that many of its buildings dating back to the Venetian Era had survived and the harbour was again thriving.

Our hosts met us in the harbour as we descended from the local bus and we walked the brief half mile from the harbour further south to their house, pleasantly situated over a small bay. I have to admit that we were rather surprised as they showed us to our room. This was a large piece of cardboard in which their refrigerator had been delivered placed in a small olive orchard at the side of their house. After dinner, we were given pillows and blankets and wished a pleasant night.

This was the first opportunity that Annabel and I had had a chance to discuss this present state of seriously unsatisfactory affairs. Lying there looking up to a magnificent sky full of stars, I was at a loss to explain why we had been invited if they did not have a guest bedroom. Annabel had a theory that they did not like her having met her briefly when she visited Ireland. Whatever their reasons, we decided to see how things would be the next day.

They were not much different. Our hosts made sure we were fed and taken to their local little beach. We treated them to dinner in Fiscardo that night and as Annabel and I returned to our cardboard bed under the stars we decided that was that. We were obviously not really welcome.

We would leave the following day and see if we could take a boat from Fiscardo over to the neighbouring island of Ithaca, home of Homer's hero, Ulysses.

I don't think they were sorry to see us go and I never found out why they had treated us in such an inhospitable way. Back in Dublin, it was never referred to again.

Over ouzo and mezze at a local café, we managed to convince a local fisherman that it was just the day to travel over to Ithaca. He agreed and, setting off after a convivial lunch, we arrived on the west of the island in a tiny harbour in the early evening. The fisherman and the locals started a discussion at our request to find us somewhere to stay for the night. There was no accommodation in the village.

Fortunately, one of the locals remembered that an English man owned a villa close to the village and the villager's wife was the housekeeper. The owner was not due for a few days so he and his wife were sure that the owner would have been delighted to offer his hospitality for the night. You can only imagine the delight we took in a shower, bed and mattress and our eternal gratitude to someone who never, we assumed, knew that we had been there.

The following day, with much shaking of hands and cheek kissing, we boarded the local bus and set off for the ferry port at Vathy on the east of the island. Having found a bed and breakfast with the essential outside lavatory where used paper was not flushed but set aside in a basket by the toilet, (normal practice in those days) we had a three day wait for the ferry back to Corfu.

What was so enjoyable throughout our travels in Greece was the friendliness of the Greeks. On our return to Corfu, on the ferry, we met up with a wedding party, complete with the married couple, relations, friends and musicians with food and wine in abundance who insisted that we must join in. We needed no second invitation and finally put our wonderment aside at the strange behaviour of our hosts in Cephalonia.

Our last week was spent in Corfu this time centred around Glyfada. The high spot of this part of the holiday was watching Annabel water skiing on one ski across the bay. We had met up with another young English couple both of whom Annabel taught how to ski, the young girl rising up out of the water on her first run, her boyfriend took a little longer. The only one of us four who did not manage to rise out of the water was me – to my eternal shame.

Annabel was returning to Hong Kong. I was returning to London and Dublin. We were leaving at different times so it was with a sadness that is difficult to describe we said our farewells as she boarded a ferry back to Athens to meet her flight home.

I don't know why but I had a premonition that we might not see each other again. Through our early days together, the separations seemed to create more excitement to our relationship and made our time together an adventure. This time, our separation was to be of a greater length as she was not due back in England for at least a year.

As I kept waving goodbye as her ferry pulled away and set off towards Athens, and saw her waving back, I felt an unhappiness and a loss that I hoped would be bearable and temporary despite the year of our absence.

The future, as far as we were concerned, was definitely uncertain.

Returning to Dublin, it seemed that I too was facing uncertainty. I had exhausted the time allocated to me in college and needed to look for accommodation in town. Peter and Kathie gave me a bed while I looked around.

Over time, I had acquired a nodding acquaintance with the regulars at the Davy Byrnes pub and, whilst talking to one of them called Colin, he offered me a room in his small house in Hatch Lane just off Harcourt Street in walking distance to Trinity.

If I wanted to be Bohemian, I couldn't have chosen a more interesting place or more strange people. Colin's wife, Savita, was Indian and interested in mythology and astrology. They had a country house in Wicklow though I understood it was falling apart and, on the market, as, unfortunately, Colin was an alcoholic and drinking steadily through his inheritance. The sanest member of our household was their glorious Alsatian, a dog named Diarmuid (pronounced Jeer-mid) after a demi-god of Irish mythology. If he was left behind in Wicklow, probably by mistake, he would turn up, hungry and tired, at Hatch Place a day later.

I had only been there a few months during which time I had become very friendly with Savita when she admitted that she was very worried about her husband's drinking. If I was going into college, Colin would join me for the walk but he would stop at Davy Burns and I would continue on promising to pick him up on the way home. This, of course, meant a drink or two before I could convince him to come back with me.

Just behind Hatch Place ran Harcourt Terrace, the home of Michael MacLiammoir and his partner in life and in business Hilton Edwards. Through a meeting in the Soup Bowl, I had met them and their business manager Brian Tobin.

Brian was an extremely good-looking man, tall, dark and handsome and we became very good friends. He was by then,

I think, divorced from his wife and they had two young daughters. He and his wife were from Galway and I understood that his wife had kept one daughter in Galway and Brian had come with the other daughter, Valerie, to Dublin. I think he would agree with me that he was not the most competent of fathers so Michael and Hilton had taken Valerie into their home and virtually became her parents.

If they were having a party or a celebration, they were often kind enough to invite me and, through them, I enjoyed the company of most of the whole theatrical community of Dublin both homosexual and heterosexual. You couldn't have asked for more entertainment through gossip and scandal than were offered by this merry band.

I have mentioned that Michael MacLiammoir's most famous work as both writer and actor was his one-man show 'The Importance of Being Oscar', a commentary on the life and works of Oscar Wilde. What I may not have mentioned is that he had a wicked sense of humour and one night caused me the most embarrassment I think I have ever suffered.

Michael was performing the show in London and invited me to join them one night after the show for dinner. I was to come to the stage door where Brian would bring me up to the wings to wait for the great man to end the show and accept his applause. As the curtain came down for the last time, a phalanx of young gay actors rushed on to the stage to surround their idol. Their idol turned to where I was in the wings, beckoned me with a wave of his hand and called me over with the words, 'Peter, darling'.

If I could have fallen with mortification through the stage floor, I would have done so but I had to approach Michael to be kissed on both cheeks and to hear from the chorus in whispers, 'Who is that queen, dear?', 'Is she a new one? He apologised at dinner but said it was just too good to miss seeing my horrified face. It had made his night for him. I suppose it had made the night for me, too. It gave me a memory of an extraordinary man – not to be forgotten.

Years later, Valerie and I were talking about her past and she was actually asking me to tell her more about her father. She believed that he had had an affair with Michael. I said that it had never crossed my mind that he might have been homosexual or bisexual as all the time that I knew him he was a very accomplished lover of quite a few women that we both knew – and probably a few more that I didn't know. I explained to her that I always thought that the longevity of his and Michael's relationship was because Michael could not seduce him but perhaps hoped that one day he might.

Winter was approaching fast and Savita was becoming seriously worried about her husband's alcoholism as was I. My good friends John and Helen, now married, were negotiating with a Mrs Ward to rent a three bedroomed maisonette in Monkstown south of Dublin on the road to Dun Laoghaire and suggested that, if the negotiations were successful, I should leave the madness of Hatch Place and come and live with them. "Just let me know when," I replied.

Michael MacLiammoir in a theatrical pose

Savita had called on their Parish priest for his help who, in turn, had recommended a psychiatrist who specialised in alcoholism – a busy man in those days. His recommendation was that Colin should be brought for in-house treatment to his sanatorium in the outskirts of north Dublin near Clontarf. Colin refused point blank.

Savita's solution was that I should drink Colin under the table and, when he was unconscious, we could load him into my car and drive him out to the sanatorium. I thought this was a crazy scheme but Savita was now desperate so I agreed. I found it very difficult to pretend during our mammoth drinking session that I was matching him drink for drink knowing that the worst part of the evening was yet to come – the drive through Dublin at night and out to Clontarf with an unconscious man in the back and a troubled wife by my side.

However, we succeeded, so in the early hours of the morning we manhandled Colin's unconscious body out to the car. We just couldn't get him into the back seat but just managed to lift him into the boot and set off. Of course, it was bitterly cold and raining.

I suppose it took about forty minutes to drive to the sanatorium. Once there, we rang the bell and two attendants came out to the car. I opened the boot and Colin woke up.

His first words were, "Where the fuck am I?" His next words were, "Who the fuck are these people?" And then, "Peter, what are we doing here? Take me home."

The attendants explained that they had no authority to accept someone who was refusing to enter. If he had been unconscious, they could have accepted him but no longer. We had no alternative but to drive him back home. Fortunately, only Savita and I had a clear memory of the night's events.

It was not long after this little adventure that I moved out to live with John and Helen in Monkstown. I heard from Savita that Colin did not live much longer and, after his death, she returned to her family in India. I only hope some friend looked after the Alsatian. He deserved better.

After two years in college and the madness of Hatch Lane, it was a delight to come to a three bedroomed maisonette set in a corner of a pleasant square called Belgrave Square. Not quite London but, to my mind, pretty close. Belgrave Square was only minutes from a popular bathing beach called

Seapoint and not far from the centres of Blackrock and Dun Laoghaire and, perhaps, a thirty-minute drive from the centre of Dublin.

Our arrangement was that we would share the basic outgoings on the basis of a third each and run a kitty for food and drink. This suited me as it seemed to be in my favour as Helen was very generous with her hospitality and somewhat forgetful on entering her bills.

I have mentioned earlier that having played rugby against the police force, known as 'Guards', they could be very pleasant but they were, under normal circumstances, figures to fear. They were big and they played strictly by the rules.

One night, it must have been after one in the morning, having finished an evening's work in the Soup Bowl with a glass of wine or two, I set off for home. It was a wicked night, rain bucketing down. As I approached Blackrock, a figure stood out from the pavement and flagged me down. Through the torrents of rain, I saw it was a Guard. I suddenly thought had I had two or, perhaps, more glasses of wine? It was all I needed to be taken in to the local police station suspected of being drunk.

The Guard pulled me over so I opened my window.

"Anything wrong, officer?" I asked.

"Yes," he replied. "This bloody awful weather. Are you in a hurry?"

"No," I replied.

"Then, would you mind, sir, if I sat in the car for ten minutes, had a cigarette and a rest from this damned rain?"

"It would be a pleasure. Come on in."

We both lit up and discussed life in general for a good fifteen minutes. From then on, whenever we met in the early morning, rain or shine, he would flag me down and we would enjoy a cigarette and a chat together.

Towards the end of the year, John and Helen explained that they planned to visit India and travel for most of the following year. Would I be interested in taking over the house until their return? I said I would be delighted so thought of whom I might find to join me in this new adventure. My first thought was Brian Tobin. He was living vicariously, moving from one flat to another and, if he did join me, he would at least have stability for a year. He may, though, not like being half an hour from the centre of town.

However, when I proposed it to him, he jumped at the chance. Two down, so now I needed to find a third.

I had returned to London for Christmas and had been down to visit Bon, his sister, Lisa, and their parents who lived in Cholsey in Oxfordshire. Bon's father was the local vicar and one of the holiest men I have ever met with nothing but gentleness in his behaviour. He was able to alleviate pain through touch and thought, and was often called to hospices to help those in terminal pain.

Years later, when he was dying, I visited him in hospital where his family were gathered. Within a few days, he would be celebrating his fiftieth wedding anniversary to Mary, his wife. By sheer will power, he stayed alive until a few minutes into the morning of their anniversary. It was just very moving and tears were difficult to contain.

I asked Bon if he knew of anyone looking for a room and he said he would check but he thought that one of his ballet dancing friends might need accommodation.

It turned out that this friend of a friend was an Australian ballet dancer joining the Irish National Ballet and the timing was perfect. His name was Jo Hayden.

We arranged to meet at six in the evening in Davy Burnes to test each other out. I must have arrived at about ten to six, ordered a drink and sat by the entrance. By six fifteen, there was still no applicant and at about twenty past, I was beginning to get worried. I did notice a slim young lady who could easily be a ballet dancer looking rather lost and obviously waiting for someone. I approached her and asked if she was waiting for Peter Hunt, perhaps to give him a message. "Are you Peter?" she asked.

"Yes," I replied. In a noticeable Australian accent, she replied, "A pleasure to meet you, I am Jo Hayden."

My surprise was complete as I explained to her that no one had told me that she was a female. I had just assumed that she was a male. She joined me in a drink, we chatted for some time and mutually decided that as long as she met and approved of Brian, we had the third member of our household.

From her point of view, when she discovered that I had a car and drove in to Dublin virtually every day and that her dance studio was on route, she could see her travel arrangements being sorted out as well. If not, there was an excellent bus service.

You may or you may not have been wondering how my relationship was developing with Annabel. So, basically, was I. We seemed to be drifting apart. Our correspondence had diminished and I felt that the thousands of miles that separated us, were winning and that, as a young girl approaching her twenties, she would find a life of her own in Hong Kong. I don't think we ever confirmed this to each other. We had just drifted apart.

It was not our affair, however, that was getting everyone reaching for their newspapers. It was the Profumo affair. John Profumo was the Secretary of State for War in Macmillan's Conservative Government and married to one of the most respected stars of English cinema, Valerie Hobson. This did not stop him having a fling with a particularly photogenic eighteen-year-old called Christine Keeler who was also having affairs with a gangland villain and a Russian diplomat.

This story had all the ingredients loved by newspaper editors, (naughty politicians, models, affairs, security breaches) and when Stephen Ward, a manipulator and provider of young women who is still thought by some to have involved Prince Phillip in one or two of his parties, committed suicide, the press became even more excited.

John Profumo did not help his cause by stating in Parliament that he had had nothing to do with Christine Keeler nor her friend Mandy Rice-Davies. Investigative journalism proved that he had lied and he had to resign from parliament. Prime Minister MacMillan had trusted him and was basically broken due to the scandal. He and the Conservative party lost the general election the next year and brought in the Government of Harold Wilson.

It was now that I met a young lady, Jacqui, in the Soup Bowl who was born in Malta but whose mother, Georgia, had remarried into an Irish family and had her second family of a son and five daughters with their father Noel. They were a wonderful close family living in a rambling Georgian house out near me close to Blackrock.

She was a classic Mediterranean girl with enormous black eyes and a mass of dark hair over an attractive figure and she was, perhaps, two years younger than me. She owned and ran quite a successful boutique shop for young girls of fashion in the centre of Dublin.

People have often asked me whether I missed having siblings or a family life that they considered to be normal. I, without trying to be glib, have always answered that you don't miss what you have never had.

However, with Jacqui and her family I could see the joy a happy family can generate and I thoroughly enjoyed becoming part of their family even allowing her younger sisters to climb onto my back and treat me as their horse as they went to war with another sister on the back of their brother – exhilarating but exhausting!

Five years were suddenly coming to an end and in front of me were my final exams. There was no escape but, somehow, the whole week of exams passed and we had to wait a month for the results.

The results were about to be published when I was called in by my Italian professor to discuss my results with him. It was an interesting conversation. It seems that I had been awarded a first in English and my Italian literature papers were fine. The problem was still my grasp of the Italian language though I had improved, he admitted, over the last five years. However, he offered me this deal.

If I promised him that I would never visit Italy, never read Italian, never write Italian and never speak Italian he would give me my degree. I shook his hand with acceptance and gratitude and we parted the best of friends.

Jacqui and I had formed quite a close relationship and, though no words of a permanent relationship had ever been spoken between us, many thought that it might, should or would be on the cards.

Two events dramatically upset the applecart.

I returned to Onslow Square to be advised by my parents that in a month's time, my father was to retire and that they would be coming to live in the flat full time. I would have to find somewhere else to live. The second was even more dramatic. Annabel came back into my life. Her parents had now retired and the family had returned to London. It seemed that I was still important to her.

A choice was in front of me – Jacqui or Annabel. But there really was no choice. I would have to tell Jacqui that our relationship had been superseded.

Up to then, I had had no experience of ending relationships. I seemed to have been the one to whom this unpleasant business had been doled out. I telephoned Jacqui in Dublin and told her the news. She was distraught, so distraught that the next morning my doorbell rang and Jacqui was standing there. (Fortunately, Annabel was not in situ.) All her Mediterranean emotion came flooding out and it was a dreadful scene for both her and me. I hope I never have to go through that again because I did have every sympathy for her.

Many years later, I was called upon to remember how much she did like, even love me. She was very ill and her husband telephoned me to ask me if I would come to Dublin to see her. He said that he knew that I had been a very special part of her life and knew that she would like to see me before she died. I must admit that I thought this was very noble and understanding of him so I did travel over and spent time with them. Sadly, it was soon after this visit that she died.

I found a single bedroom flat in Sloane Court East, a rather ugly building close to the Kings Road in Chelsea. I also had an Australian friend, Barry, a fashion photographer who was desperate to find accommodation. We shared this one bedroom flat. I had the single bed; he had a camp bed hidden under the bed during the day.

Our arrangement was that if either one of us had our girlfriend back to the flat (and in Barry's case there were some stunning ones), we would hang a Kellogg's cornflake box on the outside of our door and the entrant had to go off somewhere and return when he hoped the box had been removed.

It was good fun, actually, though it could be inconvenient if one of us took too long and it was raining or snowing.

Along the corridor from my flat lived a lady with whom I often shared the lift and with whom I became quite friendly. She ran an escort agency and one day she asked me if I could help her out. It seems that one of her male escorts was ill and she needed someone to escort a client, a doctor from New York attending a medical conference in London. She had employed her services for an escort to take her to the theatre and dinner that evening.

I suppose Dr Silvers was in her mid- to late-forties, well dressed and a charming companion. We went to the theatre and to Simpsons for dinner and, as it was a very pleasant evening and she had not been to London before, I suggested that we walked back from the Strand through the West End to her hotel, the Hilton at Hyde Park. When we reached her hotel, she invited me in for a drink and we went up to the first-floor bar. I was not quite sure what I was meant to do next. I had received no instructions from management. Was I supposed to take her to bed and, if so, to be paid for it? However, I did not get any overt suggestion from her that this was supposed to happen, so after our drink, I wished her good night, and went back home.

The next day, I received in cash the refund on my expenses and a present of £40.00 and told that I had been complimented by Dr Silvers on a very pleasant evening. I said that if ever I was needed again, I would be happy to oblige. Perhaps, though, I did not do my job completely as, sadly, I was never asked to perform this service again.

Jacqui modelling one of her dresses

I have not mentioned yet that I had to find something to do. I had been interviewed in Trinity by a head hunter from the BBC and I had assumed that I would have been a perfect candidate as I had worked for Radio Hong Kong when I was living there. It turned out that he was only looking for technicians, a subject of no interest to me so the whole interview was a waste of both our times.

Whether anyone else thought that advertising was my natural bent, I obviously don't know but I thought so and I started applying to advertising agencies. Most of them did not bother to answer. It was the same with London's rugby clubs. I did not receive one answer from the five I applied to. It seems the new decade had brought in new manners – or a lack of them.

The normal occupation for those with university degrees who needed a job but seemed, like me, to be unemployable was to become a supply teacher – a fill-in when regular teachers were absent. I signed on and was sent to Latchmere primary school in Wandsworth, a school at which the headmaster was actually named Mr Hacker. The first class I was to take was Religious Instruction – pretty relevant to a non-practicing Roman Catholic to teach a classroom of 20 children about Protestantism but at least we had the same Bible.

Latchmere School was a relic of the Victorian Era but not unpleasant for all that. The main classrooms were divided by a wide corridor which ran the length of the main building. There was a main east/west road along the River Thames at the front and a tarmacked playground at the back.

After a brief lecture by the headmaster about behaviour, both mine and the children's and a warning that I was not allowed to dispense any discipline, I was sent off to classroom seven.

Twenty children of both sexes between the ages of seven and twelve, I suppose, rose to greet me – an auspicious start. I bid them good morning, told them my name and suggested that they opened their books where they had left off. There was no revolt so I assumed I was on the right path.

At the end of the day, Mr Hacker sent for me to join him in his study. I feared the worst but this meeting was, in fact, to ask me if I was free for the next three weeks as I would be needed to teach English to the same class in room seven. Obviously, this was much more up my street than Religious Instruction so I had no problem in agreeing.

Much to my surprise, I had gainful employment for almost a month and my first ever pay-cheque – suddenly a new meaning to my life! This was extended for a further three weeks.

My children were not from privileged backgrounds but they were reasonably attentive and through an inspired method for discipline that I invented, we came to a constructive understanding – so much so that we succeeded in presenting to another class our interpretation of an extract from the plays of Shakespeare.

If a pupil was misbehaving, I sent him or her out into the corridor. Eventually, the whole class ended up in the corridor so I taught out there and sent them back in again one by one as they merited it. At first, they thought this was great fun but they soon got bored so decided that they might just as well stay in the classroom. Honour was satisfied on both sides and they really became a delightful group of children to teach.

It was towards the end of my teaching career, all of six weeks, that I received an offer to be a researcher for Granada Television working from their London office in Golden Square in the heart of the West End.

I shared a ground floor office with Tim who went on to further his career in television whilst I found that the research that I was asked to do was in the most part extremely depressing.

One project I was involved in was to interview householders in the depth of the south east of London about rat and cockroach infestations in their dwellings which were, in reality, slums. The only lesson I learnt from this was to realise that there was a very different London to the part that I lived in and to be grateful for the benefits I enjoyed.

A more interesting project, to me at least, was to interview the Rockers who had been arrested for their part in the battles that used to take place between the Mods and Rockers (scooters v motorcycles) on the south coast, culminating in all-out war in Brighton. I interviewed about ten of them, all leather jacketed, tattooed and from the south of London – hard men. What I found most amusing was that, according to them, not one of them was guilty and the police were institutionally biased. They were always picked on despite the fact that they were in truth, model citizens.

None of the subjects I researched were ever made into programmes so I was very fortunate that my long-time friend from Trinity, Gay Turtle, had married a TV producer Tony Firth who produced the very successful Saturday night show called 'On the Braden Beat' for ATV, starring Bernard Braden. I was offered a job on their research team which I accepted.

I suppose we all do stupid things in life and I now committed one of my most stupid. I must have been reading too much P. G. Wodehouse whose hero, Bertie, liked to knock helmets of policemen's heads.

I must have been working 'On the Braden Beat' for some months, thoroughly enjoyable, the programme being recorded on Saturday morning to be aired on Saturday night. One Friday night with my friends John and Kerrie, I had been enjoying dinner in Mario and Franco's restaurant La Trattoria Terrazza in Romilly Street in Soho, a restaurant that had revolutionised London's idea of Italian cuisine.

We must have been the last to leave and on our way through the streets of Soho we stopped to watch a group of police raiding a night club, of sorts. I joined in with other members of the crowd jollying the police along and the next thing I knew was that my arm was up between my shoulder blades and I was being frog marched off to a Black Maria van standing by. I was arrested for foul and obscene language and obstructing the Queen's Highway.

I cannot recommend a night in the cells at West End Central on a Saturday early morning. Having been processed, I was led into a cell and locked in for the night with one excuse for a bed and one excuse for a toilet – seriously unpleasant and degrading. My fellow prisoners were even more intoxicated than I and sung and shouted to each other all night. If a policewoman passed through the cells' aisle, they filled the air with catcalls, wolf whistles and comments of a highly personal nature.

Early in the morning, we were taken from our cells and loaded into another Black Maria to be taken to the Magistrates Court nearby – magistrate in charge Mr Barraclough. Before entering the court, a policeman took me aside and advised that I should plead guilty to the charge. If I did, I would be brought in front of the magistrate before those who pleaded not guilty. If the court did not get to those pleading not guilty, they would be bound over for the weekend and sit in jail until Monday's court was in session. I had no choice but to plead guilty as I was meant to be on my way to the studio with Bernard Braden in a couple of hours. He also advised me that if I was fined and I did not have enough money to pay the fine, I must ask for time to pay. It is always given.

It was over an hour before I came before Mr Barraclough. Hearing that my address was Onslow Square in South Kensington, he looked closely at me and asked the police witness to repeat the language that I was meant to have said to provoke the charge of foul and obscene language. It was mostly Cockney slang and unintelligible to both me and the magistrate. Again, he looked very closely at the policeman with a meaningful look and then addressed me. "It seems that you have been very foolish and unfortunate but you have pleaded guilty so I have no choice. I recommend you forgo the pleasures of Soho in the early hours of the morning in future. Two pounds on each offence."

"Time to pay," was the only reply that I could think of but I did realise that I had been lucky as far as my fine was concerned due, I believe, to a comprehending magistrate who realised that this had been a stitch-up by the police.

The only problem was that I had missed my appointment with the studio and my career in television had just ended – rather unfortunately and rather too dramatically!

I was again out of work.

Life, however, does throw up some extraordinary occurrences and peculiarities. I was at a performance of a play at the Old Vic whose title I can't remember (I think it was Jumpers) when I went to the gentlemen's lavatory during an interval. Whilst there, I commented about the play to a large man who was washing his hands at the same time as me. We started to chat and he asked if I was doing anything after the play. I said that my girlfriend and I were thinking of going over to the West End for dinner. He said that he was enjoying our conversation and would I mind if he and his wife joined us for dinner. I said we would be delighted and so started a friendship that set me off on my next career.

His name was Peter Friedlander and his wife's, Rebecca. They were middle aged, entertaining and knowledgeable about theatre and the media. It turned out that he was a film producer though I am not sure that he ever produced a film. Despite this, he lived life to the full and, most important to me, he said he would introduce me to a friend of his, Eric Garrott, who ran a small advertising agency. He did and I was called in to his agency situated in Brook's Mews in the heart of Mayfair for an interview.

The agency's main accounts were BSM (the British School of Motoring), Helena Rubinstein cosmetics, Cyril Lord carpets, MEA (Middle East Airlines) and Flavel Gas Fires. There were about thirty employees spread through the arts, copy and production departments lorded over by Mr Garrott who was not a tall man but punched well above his height.

Fortunately, I had taken the precaution of reading through as many magazines and Sunday papers that I could get my hands on to see what advertising of the day looked like so I was not a complete idiot when interviewed about my thoughts on modern advertising.

I was offered a job at £600 per year as a trainee account executive which meant that I would work for a few months in each department to understand the workings of the agency. It was expected that I would eventually become an account executive charged with handling accounts and, most importantly, bringing in new business.

I was to start in the copy department headed by a fiery lady, Joan Startern and seated in an office with their lead copy writer, Alfie Golden. Alfie fascinated me. He was from the East End of London, had left school at 16 and hitchhiked around the world. He had continually self-educated himself and was just a natural copy-writer. He could see what was later called the 'Unique Selling Point' of a product and how best to attract customers to it.

Later, after he had left us and joined a larger agency, one of his most famous lines was for Cadbury's fruit and nut chocolate bar – 'The Fruit and Nut' case.

I learnt a lot from him but I was never a natural copy writer despite my only creative headline which was for MEA airlines who were hosting an equestrian event in Lebanon. My line was 'Thoroughbred flying with MEA'.

My only other claim to fame was to be involved with a team within the agency which came up with TV and magazine advertisements for Cyril Lord's carpets with the headline 'Luxury you can afford with Cyril Lord'. Unfortunately, our advertising did not stop him going bust a few years later.

What I did discover was that I was a much better writer of PR (Public Relations) articles because I had time to tell the product's story without having to find that special headline, USP or concept.

I was a gopher for the art department when I was told that we were to do a photo shoot in Annabel's night club for Helena Rubinstein's Christmas collection of cosmetic brands. The products were tastefully displayed on a beautiful long-haired white rug supplied by Mark Birley, the owner of Annabel's night club. Various labels had to be glued onto some of the products and I was commissioned to take a tin of Cowgum, a rubber solution glue beloved of art designers, to glue on the labels.

Sure enough, I tripped over the edge of the rug and spilt half a tin of glue over the rug and some of the products. I can only thank the Lord that the gum was spirit based and after an expensive bill from a Mayfair dry cleaner I returned the rug to Mark Birley without him being any the wiser.

This little adventure again was a bonus as I applied for membership and was accepted, a membership I held for close to 30 years. Annabel's had an interesting tradition concerning membership. The amount you paid in annual membership was never increased. It stayed the same as the amount you paid when you first became a member.

I had heard that there was a drug culture of hippies smoking marijuana and that the new pop groups and fashion photographers and general, rich layabouts were in to sniffing cocaine, taking LSD or both but, to be honest, I was totally unaware of it. I never came across any drugs in the nightclubs such as the Garrison that I frequented nor through contacts with my clients.

Certainly, in the advertising world in which I was gainfully employed, even though we were perhaps not a major player, our drug taking, if it can be called that, was cigarette smoking and alcohol of which, I have to admit, we consumed a lot – of both. I probably smoked at least one packet of 20 cigarettes a day and on party nights another packet. It was not too much of a financial burden as a packet of twenty cost 4 shillings (20p). I can remember, it was almost a reflex action that if the phone rang, I lit a cigarette even though there was one burning in the ashtray. Just about everybody smoked and we thought no more about it.

I was enjoying my days in advertising but I was not sure I was going anywhere. I also realised that if I was to succeed, I had to bring in new clients and I had no background from which to deliver them. My contacts in Dublin were virtually useless as they did not include vibrant companies. I had no longer any contacts in Honk Kong and I had no knowledge of the financial world of the booming City of London.

Further, I had not kept in touch with any of my old school friends from five years ago, none of whom seemed to have achieved much anyway.

From my days in the Soup Bowl in Dublin, I had met and enjoyed the company of a London restaurateur and wine buff called David Wolfe. He owned a restaurant in Abingdon Road off Kensington High Street called, with great originality, Wolfe's.

He was not a tall man but was married to Ingrid, a tall, statuesque blonde whose love, other than David, was her Persian cat. It was just as well that they owned a restaurant because the cat only ate smoked salmon, prawns or shrimps.

With his Swiss chef, Claude Bonny, the restaurant soon developed a reputation for food that reflected the new trends for fine or experimental cooking with traditional common sense. It attracted a clientele that included the stars of the enormously popular TV series 'The Avengers', Diana Rigg and Patrick MacNee, film stars and fashion models such as Terence Stamp who was courting Jean Shrimpton, at that time the world's top model, as well as successful businessmen and professionals.

As Claude ruled the kitchen, staff of four, so Umberto, an Italian with presence, ruled front of house. Service was impeccable and the wine list well-chosen by the enthusiasm and experience of David Wolfe.

Annabel and I quite often enjoyed an evening here when we felt that we had something to celebrate.

David invited me to join him to be trained as his second in command while learning the business of both his restaurant and his wine company. He offered me a starting salary of twice the amount that I was earning at Garrott's. This was not an offer I could refuse. It would open up a whole new world just there to be discovered.

I am happy to say that Eric Garrott was not too pleased when I handed in my notice and, later, was one of the few employers that I have ever worked for who actually contacted me to ask me to return to a larger advertising agency that he had acquired. He even threw in a new Triumph Stag motorcar as an inducement to complement my salary.

I was not tempted despite the offer of the Triumph Stag motorcar.

And so, to Wolfe's in Abingdon Road.

I was not prepared, however, to find just how hard running and working in a restaurant proved to be.

I began in the office at about eight in the morning to do the banking from the night before and then helped in the kitchen until the lunchtime trade began. It was then, under the training of the watchful eye of Umberto, that I started life as a 'commie' waiter, virtually the lowest form of life in a restaurant as the kitchen porter (KP) is in the kitchen.

The restaurant operated the 'tronc' system of distributing tips. It was a very traditional system that rewarded longevity and seniority. The head waiter took 50%, the Sommelier took 25% and the final 25% was shared amongst the rest of the waiting staff, perhaps four or five of us at a busy time. When I questioned the system as being unfair, Umberto explained that it was a system created to set a goal of achievement for the young and a reward for those who were good enough to last the course. It was difficult to argue with the logic.

After a while, I moved into the kitchen and was given the responsibility for preparing the starters and desserts under the care of both, Claude, head chef and his number two, Luigi, a football mad Italian whose speciality was the fish courses at which he excelled.

I have never been particularly interested in football but working in a restaurant with both an Italian headwaiter and sous chef who were enthusiastic fans of the game, it became impossible not to be involved in the World Cup, being played in England that year. We seemed to have a sweepstake going which I did not understand but we forecast the number of goals that would be scored in each match and donated a pound into the kitty. At my first attempt, I entered a rugby score, something like 18-15 to be the butt of much humour. Thereafter, I found it easier to settle for 1-2 or 3-0 depending on my mood.

As we now know, England won the World Cup, the only time that it has ever happened in my reasonably long life despite the forecasters invariably claiming that England would win each succeeding one.

Many years later, I was at a dinner at which Alan Ball was the after-dinner speaker. He was telling us about playing in the winning side and his best story featured a speech made by the manager, Alf Ramsey, before their semi-final game against Portugal. He addressed his team in the dressing room before the match by saying, "Gentlemen, this is the match we need to win. If we win this, we will win the World Cup."

They are a competent team but they have one outstanding player in Eusebio and turning to his mid-fielder Nobby Stiles, he said, "Nobby, you have to mark him." Nobby's immediate reply was, "What, Guv, for life?"

Alan Ball explained there was a sequel to this. Everywhere Eusebio went on the field, Nobby was like a terrier snapping at his feet, jostling him and making his life as difficult as possible. One of the other Portuguese players came up to Nobby and said that if he continued to carry on like this, he, personally, would knock Nobby's teeth in. Nobby replied, "Bloody difficult, mate. They are in my handkerchief, back in the dressing room."

As well as working in the restaurant, I would also set off across Hyde Park to our wine warehouse in Bayswater where I was in charge of stock, not only for the restaurant but we took orders from customers for deliveries to their homes.

I returned back for lunch service and back to the wine warehouse for the afternoon receiving deliveries then back to the restaurant, via home for a shower and change, and then back for evening service which could end up past one in the morning.

The only time I saw Annabel was when she came in for dinner or on Sundays when I was so tired that all I wanted was sympathy and sleep.

David eventually decided that the restaurant was successful enough to stop serving lunches and concentrate on the evening trade. This was a great boon and relief for me as it gave me much more leisure time; time that I was determined to enjoy.

Opposite 'Wolfe's' was a restaurant called the 'Pie qui Rit', one with which we were on friendly terms. If we or they needed something in an emergency and the other could help, we only had to cross the road. Dan, a good-looking young man of my age, was the second in command there and we soon became good friends. Dan had another good friend named Gerry Gordon, who later became Mayor of Kensington (1989–1990), a lawyer of the same age as us.

We became known as the three musketeers and, with our girlfriends, spent as much of our leisure time together, disgracefully spending as much time as we could at Gerry Gordon's mother's delightful cottage and garden in Sussex.

My parents had decided that they had had enough of London and my father wanted to live closer to his mother who was now of an age and living in Rome. However, for some reason unknown to neither me nor my mother, he did not want to live in Italy.

(I think it was something to do with there being no television reception for the BBC's weekly horse racing coverage) so they moved to Lugano in the Ticino, the Italian speaking part of Switzerland where, I suppose, there was the TV coverage and he was in striking distance of Rome.

They, very kindly, gave the apartment in Onslow Square back to me. Barry and I were more than delighted to share the flat, both now with a bedroom of our own.

Unfortunately, probably through the pressure of basically running the restaurant and wine company for David while he concentrated on writing articles about wine and promoting wine, my relationship with Annabel was not going well. We decided to split up. I am not sure who suffered most but I know that I regretted terribly that our lives just seemed to be going in different directions. I missed her terribly and found it quite difficult to even think about pursuing other girls.

Fortunately, Barry was still a fashion photographer and a chain of quite stunning young girls came and went through the apartment. There had to be some solace somewhere so I tried hard to join in and be entertained.

But, yet again, fate decided to take a hand. David and his wife separated rather unpleasantly with a lot of shouting and screaming. They were both volatile and gave full vent to their feelings fortunately not in the restaurant but I could hear them having a go at each other from their apartment above. Most of the arguments I heard seemed to concern who would keep the cat when they were divorced.

David decided that he would come back into the restaurant on a full-time basis taking over most of the roles that I had covered in his place. We also had a long chat about one of his original ideas which was to set up a second restaurant in another part of town which either he or I would run. He admitted that he had gone cold on the idea and he felt more than happy to concentrate on what he had – the restaurant and the wine company.

I thought I knew where this conversation was going but I was pleasantly surprised that I was not exactly being thrown to the wolves (ha ha).

Through a Mister Kidwai, a diplomat in the Indian High Commission, he had found out that the Commission needed a manager for the India Tea Centre, a catering and retail outlet they owned in Oxford Street, near the Bond Street Underground station in the heart of possibly the busiest thoroughfare in London. David had offered my services. It was a three-month contract whilst they waited for a new manager to arrive from India and would allow me time to seek new employment.

This was my introduction to a quite different world of catering.

The tea centre operated on three floors. The ground floor catered both for the retail of Indian teas as well as having chairs and tables for enjoying snacks, sandwiches, cakes and various flavours of tea including Assam and Darjeeling, both of which were drunk from tall glasses without milk. The first floor was the main retail area for meals whilst the basement included the kitchens, wash rooms and a couple of offices, one of which was mine.

I had two assistant managers, one lady and one man, both charming Indians, twelve waitresses, all Irish, an Italian headwaiter whose sole object in life was to make the lives of my waitresses hell by trying to pinch or squeeze their bottoms and a selection of Indian chefs in the kitchen.

On my very first morning, I received a delegation of waitresses, all complaining at the behaviour of the damned headwaiter and threatening to leave unless I manacled his hands. I called him in and told him to sort himself out or out he would be. His behaviour did improve but I had to keep at him whenever I suspected he was going to start troubling the girls again. My life was made easier in this respect in that one of the girls took to me so I had inside information when his behaviour was on the turn.

One problem that Mr Kidwai, a truly elegant and distinguished, green eyed diplomat from the North of India, explained was that I could deal with the Europeans as I thought fit but that if any of the Indians were involved, I must deal with them through my assistant managers. I assumed that being on the payroll of the high commission they had diplomatic status. It seemed a shame that it wasn't offered to me.

I had, though, managed to have collected a little nest egg so I bought myself a Triumph Spitfire sports car. Quite the man about town now!

This was in July, one of the hottest July months on record. Looking out from my office I saw one of our chefs going towards the exit wearing an overcoat. *Strange,* I thought, in this weather so called him and the two managers into my office and asked them to ask him to take off his coat.

With a great deal of complaining, he eventually did and around his body were three cords of string from which chicken carcasses hung. I realised we had a problem with staff theft from the kitchens.

He was reprimanded but allowed to stay on until I again caught him stealing chickens by feeding them through one of the tiny kitchen windows to a confederate on the fire escape outside. This time, I was informed, he was fired by the Indian authorities and, presumably, sent home.

Obviously, I had been giving some thought to the problem of life after my three-month contract expired. Did I want to try to go back to advertising?

No, not really. Did I want to try and stay in the Catering trade? No, not really. From my advertising days, I had looked fondly and taken an interest in our clients' companies having dealt with their marketing men. Marketing seemed to involve not only advertising and public relations but every activity of creating and selling products. I contacted some of the marketers I had worked with and picked their brains learning as much as I could from them.

In one of the Sunday papers, there appeared an advertisement for young marketing executives to join a company then called Brown and Polson, famous as manufacturers of cornflour and blancmange. I applied, went through two interviews and was offered a job as a trainee product manager.

The company's head office was at Claygate, near Esher, in Surrey, set in the countryside with its own tennis court and swimming pool, a canteen and situated close to a village green with cricket ground. The offices were modern and air conditioned but I was not to see them for some time. I was assigned to a sales manager, given a Ford Cortina, a week's training in sales and sent off to run my sales territory which ran from Woolwich, south of the Thames to Bromley in north Kent, an area totally foreign to me but in which I had to quickly find my way around. Fortunately, in those days, traffic was light and nothing like the nightmare it is today.

These were the days when the supermarkets were coming into their own, dominating the old chain stores and co-ops though there were still many independent stores trying to compete by joining wholesale marketing brands such as SPAR or hanging on for dear life. I had many of these on my patch.

It was quite obvious that self-service and the supermarket format was the future. I can still remember the old Sainsbury's stores in my mother's time when she would queue at each counter first for dairy, then for meat, then for fish, then for grocery – a tedious procedure to say the least.

I also remember one of the features of the department stores that fascinated me. Above the sales counters, there was a network of wires coming from a machine behind each counter and leading to an account's office on a mezzanine floor.

When you paid for your purchase, the sales assistant placed your money and the invoice in a small container, pulled a switch and with a whoosh, the container shot off up the wires to the office. Your change returned by the same route. It was magic and just proves that progress may be great but not everything is for the best.

I developed my own theory of being a good salesman or rep. You either sold yourself first and then your goods or the goods first and then yourself. The first suited me best and, though I say it myself, I surprised everyone by being quite good at it and beating my targets each month.

It was not always easy. I had a very difficult co-op manager in Woolwich, a big man, hard as nails and quite intimidating. Other than our cornflour products, we carried Knorr packet soups with which we were trying to get a share of the soup market dominated by Heinz and Campbell's tinned soups.

Our marketing people had designed a wire stand to erect at the end of a gondola, the name given to a type of shelving unit within the shops. Each wire stand took about 12 varieties of packet soups in its four layers of shelves. Each packet of soup had to be priced and placed on the shelves of the unit.

My co-op manager refused to have one in his store. I decided differently so, after he had gone back into his office, I erected the stand, priced the soups, filled the stand and placed it in all its glory at the end of a gondola. The next thing I knew, he had picked up both me and the stand in his huge arms and deposited us both out in the street. Packets of soup were everywhere.

Right, I thought, *war has been declared.* So, I picked myself up, re-made the stand and took it back in and placed it again at the end of the gondola. He watched me then called me over to his office.

"I will give you one thing," he said. "You might sound posh but you've got bottle. I will give it one week. If anything sells off of it, we'll see." We shook hands. I returned a week later and he told me he couldn't believe it. Not all the flavours were popular but he had sold out of Minestrone within three days. I actually missed calling on him when I left the life of a travelling salesman.

After about three months running my patch, I was called back to head office and, under the watchful eye of Fred Perry, the head of marketing, I became a product manager for Brown and Polson Cornflour and Blancmange. As we had 90% of the market, this was not, at first, a challenging task.

One of my colleagues was in charge of marketing cornflour internationally. He told me that they kept receiving enormous orders for cornflour from one African country and they could not understand why. Eventually, it turned out that the ladies of the country made it into a paste which they used as a contraceptive. How successful this method was, we never found out but the orders kept coming.

I soon realised that the traditional lifestyle of the housewife cooking for her family from locally produced food was on the decline due, of course, to the influence of supermarkets and a proliferation of processed, ready-made meals.

Our sales of blancmange were declining naturally and we deleted all but two of the most popular flavours when in 1967 Bird's produced and televised heavily 'Angel Delight'. It dominated the market and relegated our product to the second division.

However, by this time, our company had been taken over by Corn Products, a large American corn-based conglomerate and they decided to launch their range of Gerber baby foods, sold in glass jars, into the UK market dominated by Heinz with their tinned products.

I was appointed as the brand manager.

We began our launch by concentrating on chemists and offering them exclusivity to allow them to compete with the supermarkets. We also had to try and convince the Americans (particularly difficult to deal with as they thought they knew best about everything) that some of their flavours like PBJ (peanut butter and jam) would not be immediate hits in the UK market. Eventually, we reduced the number of flavours that were originally presented to us to a more manageable number and, hopefully, more acceptable to the British babies' taste.

Heinz did not lie down. They began by launching a campaign insinuating that glass jars were dangerous. This had a rather unpleasant consequence.

We began to receive a few complaints from mothers that the jar had broken and the glass had cut their baby's mouth. As you can imagine, I had to take this seriously and I visited every complainant. I regret to say that in almost every case, it turned out that the family itself had broken the jar and used this as an excuse to try and get compensation from us.

The world is not necessarily an honest place!

Also, we had to go back on our word to the chemists. The power of the supermarkets was becoming so strong that we had to sell to them to survive and could no longer give exclusivity to the chemists. Both the sales director and I felt ashamed when we had to visit the head buyers of chemists such as Boots to explain why we had to do what we had to do. This was definitely not one of my happier moments in my business life so far!

Our activities as brand managers were overseen by Fred Perry, the marketing group manager but administered by a retired RAF air traffic controller, Clement Tuesbury, nicknamed Clem. He and I had our moments when he objected to certain areas of expenditure which he considered frivolous but he was responsible for introducing me to the Kingston rugby club and the local cricket club. Another of his attributes was that he refereed our local rugby games as well as umpiring our village green cricket matches.

It was not often that he spoke of his wartime activities but he did once tell me about an extraordinary feat in which he was involved as an RAF air traffic controller.

Information arrived at his base that the Bismarck, one of Germany's magnificent modern battleships, was entering the English Channel. His squadron of Fairey Swordfish, a biplane torpedo bomber which should have been retired as obsolete in 1939, was selected to attack the Bismarck.

Clem and his fellow controllers knew that this was a suicide mission and could only listen nervously to their radios as the squadron set off. To their intense surprise, the squadron returned having dealt enough damage to the steering controls of the battleship so that the Royal Navy could finish it off the next morning.

The success of this mission came about due, in great part, to the aircraft flying so slowly. The German gunners had set their fire control predictors for faster aircraft so their shells exploded before reaching the Swordfish. At the same time, their flak weapons could not depress enough to hit the low flying Swordfish. It was an extraordinary achievement for the squadron.

The Swordfish aircraft managed to survive the war and they were responsible for more sunk enemy tonnage than any other British aircraft. Sadly, the German Messerschmitt fighters were to savage their attacks later in the war. Their exploits and their pilots' heroism should be remembered in line with those of the Mosquitos, Hurricanes and Spitfires.

Another of my university activities – that of being an amateur actor, was revived in a strange way. After a particular muddy game of rugby, Clem approached me and asked me if I knew anything about acting.

I said that I had acted at university but not since. Would I then be able to help out the Surbiton Amateur Dramatic Society called the Ember Players who had lost their leading man with only two weeks to go before opening night? Could I help? I said I would give it a go and, sure enough with enormous help from my friend Kerrie with learning my lines, I played Tom Wrench in a play called 'Trelawny of the Wells'.

This was followed by playing the lead role as a professor in a strange play called 'The Burning Glass'. In both, I received reasonable critiques but I did not see stardom staring me in the face.

In those days, and perhaps still today, we developed close relationships with our suppliers – lunches being a regular feature of mutual hospitality more on their part rather than ours. I became particular friends with our supplier of printing material. He introduced me to one of the secondary Esher teams where I played when not required at Kingston.

In those days, Esher was a premier league club so we had access to Twickenham for the Internationals and for the Middlesex sevens. We could park in the car park, have a mobile bar and a barbecue and walk in and out of the stadium and sit anywhere for the Sevens. Seating was by ticket for the Internationals which, even then, were virtual sell-outs.

My usual Kingston team was rather lower down the divisions but I enjoyed playing for both and enjoying the camaraderie and hospitality at both clubs.

My print supplier's name was Michael Gordon and I became so friendly with him and his wife Jane that they honoured me by asking me to be godfather to their son. After his birth, I arranged for a case of Gerber baby food to be delivered to their home. Somewhere, somehow, the instruction got screwed up and a container arrived at their house and unloaded half a container full of baby food. Regrettably, their son took an instant dislike to it.

Well, you can't win them all!

It was at a lunch with Michael one day that I had a bright idea. We would start a greetings card company and from somewhere in the depths of my mind arose the company name 'Pretty Fair'. The concept was based on the success of Playboy magazine, a magazine that's popularity was based mainly, as far as I could see, on humour and the attractiveness of the female form.

We would have three directors/partners, me as financier and copy writer, Michael as printer and we met a fashion photographer Paul Carapetian who was enthusiastic to join us.

Starting with our first card whose front face had the headline 'This could be your record year' with a photograph of an attractive, lightly clothed model standing by a Wurlitzer Jukebox. You opened the card and inside was the wording 'If everything comes off as you expect' and the lady suitably undressed.

We produced eight cards with the rather weak copy lines but very attractive models. They were:-

This could be your record year…If everything comes off as you expect.

A touch of light relief…Can open up quite a proposition.

There are two sides to every problem…Resolving this one could give you a…

Just the odd adjustment…Could make this a most revealing year.

A leg up and over…Is a step in the right direction.

A fresh approach…Could bring things bubbling over.

A bit behind this year…Then keep abreast the next.

A little of what you fancy does you good…More of it would mean a…

We were fortunate to find a stationery wholesaler prepared to distribute them for us. We started off with a modicum of success but then disaster struck.

We had launched just at the time that Mary Whitehouse started her national campaign against what she described as the wave of pornography taking over the media in Britain involving cinema, stationery and television. Our cards were moved from eye line in our retailers to the top shelf, the area where the more hard-core magazines were sold. Our sales died a death and my first essay into entrepreneurship died with it.

Our friendship ended tragically. Michael had been to an International rugby match at Twickenham and after the match had left the stadium to cross the busy A316 that ran across the front of the stadium. He was talking to a friend and stepped out into the road. He was hit by a car and died almost instantly. Twickenham, at the next international, held a short silence in memory of him.

After swanning around in my social life, in which I had kept in touch with my Air Lingus girl friends from my Dublin days, I had had a short affair with a mad but delightful air hostess from Galway called Claire. I must admit she was a great companion but not easy to live with, though she proved to be surprisingly supportive when one of those things in life occurred that, if I was to live again, I would not repeat.

In 1967, the breathalyser was introduced. I decided that I wanted to be breathalysed – Lord alone knows why. Claire and I spent an evening in the West End, leaving the Garrison club towards 2 am. I decided that not only would I drive home but I would circle the statue outside Buckingham Palace until stopped and breathalysed.

The pass mark for sobriety was a percentage of alcohol in the blood of 40. I was recorded at 202.

I was taken to the police station accompanied by Claire, processed (which took over two hours and during this annoyance she sat by me) and we were sent home to return to the magistrate's court the next day. I noticed the magistrate looking up at me over his glasses as he read my address and he gave me one of those looks that show serious disapproval of such behaviour by young men of my age.

He then asked me if I had anything to say. A moment of madness swept over me and I replied, "No, sir, except it is the only examination that I have passed with a distinction." No smile met this attempt at humour.

"Fined £40 pounds and licence suspended for 15 months." The normal punishment was one year's suspension. I just had to assume that the extra three months were added on for impertinence.

I did try to drive as little as possible during this period but if I had to drive, I fortunately had retained my Irish licence but, in truth, I really only used this one if I was out of the UK.

Claire sensibly left me to it and a little later I was introduced by an old school friend to a young lady called Hope.

Through Hope, I was introduced to a style of life that I had not known before – the style of country life, jam sessions, county charity balls shows and point to points. Hope's father was an MP for an area east of Bath in Somerset and the family lived in a beautiful Georgian house in the village of Batheaston.

The family was of Canadian descent and Edwin (Ted), Hope's father, had fought with the Allies during the war, been successful in business in the City, was a senior Freemason, a frequent contestant on the radio show, the Brain's Trust, as well as an MP. Oddly enough, he was also an excellent drums player.

His wife was charming and the perfect companion to her husband's career. They had two daughters, Hope, the elder and Sarah, the younger. Their London apartment was just round the corner from mine in South Kensington. So, there were advantages for both of us and we began, as they say, to start going steady.

Edwin, whilst an MP, had been responsible for relationships between the UK and the Caribbean and, on one of his trips to Jamaica, had become good friends with a family of sugar plantation owners in Jamaica – the McConnells. One member of the family was sending his three sons to school in England and asked Edwin if he would be a guardian to them. This, he was pleased to do.

There were many attractions at Batheaston. Quite often, on a Sunday night, Ted would set out the drums and Chris Barber, then the most famous jazz musician of the time (promoter of Lonnie Donegan and skiffle music), members of his band and Millicent Martin, a famous singer, would gather in the drawing room and, with Ted on the drums, play the evening through.

We would be invited to hunt balls, to point-to-point racing and to garden parties and countywide charity events. I would meet government ministers at dinner and be introduced by Ted to the Tory hierarchy. This was balanced by a swimming pool and tennis court and delightful grounds at their welcoming home.

About the same time that I started going out with Hope, I heard that my grandmother had died and that my parents were to leave Switzerland. They returned to England and bought a house in Folkestone on the Downs overlooking the Channel.

However, my parents' stay in Folkestone was short lived.

As a result of the Labour victory in 1964, the economy was going from worse to worst with the unions not helping by fighting for a life style that was no longer viable.

I have already mentioned the restriction to £50 per year for foreign travel but to people like my parents there was worse to come. The Chancellor introduced so many taxes that for those with even moderate savings, the income tax demanded came to 110% in the pound – an assault on savings and wealth that had never even been dreamt of by past governments.

It was a year before, 1963, that under the Government of Harold MacMillan, the Government had approached the European consortium known as the Common Market to join the founder five European countries including France and Germany. This application was vetoed by France's President De Gaulle. In 1967, under Harold Wilson's government, Britain again tried to join. Again, the application was vetoed by De Gaulle. It was not until 1973 on the 1st of January that Britain, Ireland and Denmark succeeded in joining the European Community, later to become the European Union.

My parents sold their house and moved to Jersey in the Channel Islands, a sort of half-way house between England and France, an area outside the British tax system but still within the sterling currency zone. The income tax in the island was a more moderate 20% and even more advantageous as far as my father was concerned, he could receive BBC television and his weekly dose of horse racing.

Jersey is a very attractive island though not that large at nine miles from west to east and five miles from north to south and supporting in those days a population of some 50,000. The north coast is defined by 300-foot cliffs melding into a good agricultural plain descending to beautiful bays in the south and west. It has excellent air and ferry routes to Britain and to France, its nearest neighbour, a mere 20 miles away.

The house my parents eventually bought was called Sous le Chene (under the oak). It was close to the church and the manor in the most north-westerly parish, St Ouen, (pronounced like the Spanish Juan). It was three-bedroomed with a small, manageable garden for which they took on the services of a gardener with the appropriate name of Peter Rabet (rabbit). The local village was half a mile away and St Helier, the capital town was about five miles away to the southeast. It suited them well as did the gentler life of a country parish.

One of the 8 Pretty Fair cards

On my first visit to our new home and, having settled in and found my bearings, I set off to the nearest good golf course (of which there were two, La Moye in the west and the Royal in the east), La Moye being the obvious choice.

I explained to the steward that I was new to the island so knew no one who might propose me. He called over one of the members who was in the lounge and introduced me to him, a Major Bobby Peel. He then gave me this wonderful interrogation.

"I understand you would like to become an overseas member. Where do you live?"

"In London, sir."

"Where in London?"

"South Kensington, sir."

"Where in South Kensington?"

"Onslow Square, sir."

"Bloody good address. We need more chaps like you in the club. Give the steward a fiver and I'll make sure you are a member within the week." Sure enough, I had a telephone call within the week from the secretary that on receipt of my membership fee, I would immediately be a member. I went to pay that afternoon.

Incidentally, on my next visit to the clubhouse, the steward Nigel and I began a friendship which is still current to this day.

It was not long after this that I received a telephone call from a Major Bonn in Jersey asking if I would give a lecture on mail order to a business school that he ran on the island. He would pay me a fee, my flight and a night in a hotel in St Brelade's Bay positioned on Jersey's premier south facing beach. I never did find out how he found my name but, at that time, I was involved in direct mail marketing.

Having given my lecture, I was seated for lunch in the restaurant and, at the next table, were two young men and their father. We started chatting and it turned out that the family was a Jewish family from London. The day before, the younger of their two sisters also married and after the wedding the mother told her father that she was leaving him to start her own life, as to date, she had done nothing but dedicate her life to him and her four children and received little from him in return.

He was devastated, so his sons had brought him over to Jersey to take his mind of this family tragedy. They were going to go round the island after lunch and asked whether I would like to join them. I readily agreed.

We set off in their car and, to my surprise, headed to the airport. By going round the island, they did not mean in the car but in their aircraft. It was a unique way for me to take a tour of the island which I now called home.

Sadly, I never heard from the family again but have always hoped that the father and mother were re-united. Well, I can but hope for a romantic or, at least, an agreeable family conclusion.

Hope, looking rather formal for a magazine shoot

Returning to London, Hope informed me that one of the McConnell boys from Jamaica, Stewart, had reached his 21st year and he and three of his cousins had decided to have a combined 21st birthday party. They had chosen a country club reasonably near Kingston and Spanish Town and invited the two Leather girls. My position as boy-friend had been explained and I was included in the invitation.

This trip was to have a profound influence on my future and introduced me to a family who became and still are life-long friends. How history can repeat itself! Ted had been guardian to the three McConnell boys when they were at school in England. In due course, I was to become guardian to at least six of the family's children when they also were sent to school in England.

Hope, Sarah and I arrived in Jamaica the day before the party to be met by David, the eldest of the three McConnell boys and his wife, Faye, and taken to their home in Sligoville, in the mountains above Bog Walk virtually in the middle of Jamaica and above the major route from the south to the North from Spanish Town to Ocho Rios. From the moment we arrived, I began to appreciate Jamaican hospitality. We were met at the door by their house boy with rum punches just to set us up for the rest of the evening. This included a splendid dinner featuring Jamaican specialities which always seemed to include a heavy dose of rice and potatoes as well as a further four vegetable and a rich dessert. A final glass of rum and we were ready for bed.

The next morning, I awoke, not feeling my best, to find their two children Peter and Terry standing at the end of my bed. They explained that they had instructions from their father to come over and rub my head with Bay Rum, this being their father's favourite cure-all after a late night. Having been suitably massaged, I had to agree with him and regret that, so far, I had no children to whom I could teach this delightful method of being woken up and set up for the day.

Our day was spent by taking seats in a Land Rover and being driven around the family's sugar estates in Bog Walk culminating in visiting the house where the McConnell boys were brought up but now owned by a neighbouring family of farmers. One day, David assured me, he would buy the house and bring it back into the family.

It was only later that I discovered that the house had been the scene of a dreadful family tragedy. The boys' mother had been murdered in the drive by her Jamaican driver while he was high on drugs and alcohol. No one ever discovered why he killed her as she was recognised for her charity work and her support for the local community.

As you can imagine, this left a permanent impression on the family who became overtly conscious of security and their family's safety. They all, at all times, carried guns.

The birthday party started at around 7 pm and its setting was stunning as it was given in Caymanas, an old colonial style golf club with views out over the course, over sugar cane fields and on to the Caribbean Sea.

It looked as if every member and friend of the McConnell family were present, perhaps 300 hundred people, mainly descendants of European immigrants who had come to Jamaica some centuries earlier to be involved in sugar, in trade, in the military or some as missionaries. The guest list was a reflection of this immigration melange as it included Irish, Scottish, Italian, English, Syrian, Jews, Chinese, Indian and Africans – a real Colonial hotchpotch. It was interesting to notice that the structure of their society seemed to be based on wealth not colour. If you could afford it, you were a part of it.

Our first home in Jersey, Sous le Chene

Reggae music blared out from a live band interspersed with a disc jockey. The flow of liquor was constant served by attentive waiters who remembered what you were drinking and then to dinner. Tables heaving with Jamaican delicacies were set around dining tables laid out on the verandas. After a few speeches which, to be honest, were quite difficult to understand as they were mostly given in rich Jamaican accents, the party began in earnest with dancing for those inclined, and for others, the luxury of being waited on hand and foot whilst sitting with friends and family enjoying all the local gossip.

It was about 5 am when we left to drive back to our home in the hills with the hope that the McConnell children would repeat their magic with the Bay Rum head massage later in the morning.

For the weekend, we had been invited to join David's two brothers Peter and his wife Joan and their youngest brother Stewart at their seaside home on the north coast, a house called Leisure Lee positioned on a hillside just above a beautiful bay called Discovery Bay.

It was so named as it was claimed that it was here that Christopher Columbus first landed in Jamaica.

Before leaving England, Ted had taken me aside and explained some of the McConnell family's history. He explained that we would spend most of our time with David and Faye and his younger brother Peter and his wife Joan who ran a famous sugar estate called Worthy Park located in a stunning valley plain in the hills above Bog Walk where we were staying with David. He also explained that Joan did not suffer fools gladly, was very bright and well-read. This intellectual acumen was perfected by blonde hair, blue eyes, a lissom figure and, like everyone else, a facility to switch between Jamaican patois and traditional English, though spoken with a lilting and charming accent.

The journey to the north-side of the island and to Discovery Bay was a further adventure in itself. We left Bog Walk and headed north eventually climbing up the winding road of Mount Diablo – appropriately named as there was just room for two lorries to pass in each direction and there were dozens of them. Towards the summit, we pulled into a parking area that featured about twenty road side stalls managed by rumbustious women clothed in multi colours selling everything from clothing, to drinks, to coconuts and bananas, to fruit and vegetable and to cooked foods browning on wayside barbecues. It was an extravaganza and extremely popular with travellers going both north or south.

We continued through the plains before descending towards Ocho Rios through Fern Gully, a gully of perhaps two miles' length with high sides, wild orchids and topped by the interwoven branches of plants and trees generating a delightful gully of shade.

At Ocho Rios, we turned left and followed the coast past St Anne's township, the waves of the Caribbean gently lapping the shore to our right, the coconut, banana and sugar plantations sweeping out to the mountains on our left until we reached Discovery Bay and turned up the hill to Leisure Lee.

Centred around its swimming pool, Leisure Lee was a four bedroomed house, open to the breezes and looking out over the sweep of Discovery Bay. To the left of the bay, there was a pier and storage facility for cargo boats that came to load with bauxite mined higher up in the hills – bauxite being the raw material from which aluminium is made and one of Jamaica's most important exports, the others being sugar and bananas and to a much smaller extent, cigars, spices and furniture.

To the right of the bay, a long arm reached out to the bay's entrance and on which various Jamaicans had begun to build their seaside houses. One of these houses had been built by Joan's younger sister Sheila and her husband Tony Hart so we had the pleasure of a base actually in the bay as well as our home at Leisure Lee.

It was at Leisure Lee that I was introduced by David to a drink new to me and one that became a firm favourite – a Bullshot. This is a concoction made from Vodka, beef consommé, lime juice and Jamaica's answer to Worcestershire Sauce called Pickapeppa. It was and is spicy, unusual and delicious and particularly suited to drinking before lunch.

It was also here that Joan and I developed a deep and lasting friendship that continues to this day. I have never understood why Ted had taken me aside to basically warn me about Joan being difficult. In over 40 years, we haven't had a cross word but rather we have had many an adventure with her husband, family and their friends.

For our return to Worthy Park, we were asked if we would like to take the country route to the estate rather than back over Mount Diablo.

Just a small selection of the McConnell family

We agreed and set off to St Anne's Bay where we turned right and climbed up and over the mountain range that looked down on the bay. The views were stunning, not only down over the higgledy piggledy houses but over the verdant landscape and the blue of the ocean. This changed to wilder country as we went across the plains of Moneague and then into narrow windy roads along valley edges, homes to small farmers whose children either stared at us in awe or waved frantically as we drove slowly by. Eventually, we began a descent into a wide valley completely covered in cane fields, a herd of grazing cattle, a factory, a housing compound and the workers' village known as Lluidas Vale. This was the Worthy Park sugar estate.

Peter managed the plantation and Owen Clarke, his uncle, managed the factory. Our time was spent in lazy delight, either sunning by Owen's pool, taking tours around the estate, playing golf on their nine-hole golf course or playing bridge of an evening. A special trip was a drive down to Hunt's Bay where Peter kept a splendid Hatteras power boat named by Peter, definitely with tongue in cheek; NO PROBLEM. One evening, we sped out into Kingston Bay and across to Port Royal to alight into Gloria's, a waterside restaurant, to enjoy fried fish, bammies (cassava flatbreads) and other local delicacies washed down with Red Stripe beer and/or wine.

On our return to Worthy Park, our hosts explained that they had a further expedition for our final weekend. We were to go the north east of the island, an area less known to mass tourism and one wilder than many others. We were off to Port Antonio with David and Peter, their wives and their youngest brother, Stewart.

Between Ocho Rios and Port Antonio is the townlet of Oracabessa and it is there we went in convoy driving through the twisty, pot-holed roads down through the wooded and green mountainsides until we met the coast. At Oracabessa, we turned right to follow the road along the Caribbean.

This area was the one chosen by Ian Fleming and Noel Coward in which to make their holiday homes.

Ian Fleming's holiday home is called Goldeneye. It is a fifteen-acre estate in which his house was built on the edge of a cliff overlooking his own private beach. Though it is referred to as his holiday home, it is here that many of his James Bond novels were written and, as everyone knows, Jamaica was chosen as the island setting for his novel 'Dr No' the first James Bond film which starred Sean Connery and Ursula Andress.

The estate has now been developed by Chris Blackwell of Reggae music fame as a hotel and elegant resort featuring private villas, cottages and beach huts.

Further along the coast are the summer houses of Noel Coward, perhaps one of England's greatest entertainers of the 20th century. He was a playwright, composer, actor, director and singer famous for his wit and flamboyance. By the beach is his seaside villa, Blue Harbour, but his main estate is higher up in the hills built in order to enjoy the cooler breezes.

His house, Firefly, was once the home of the notorious privateer and pirate of the 17th century, Henry Morgan. It is said that from here he could see any hostile vessels sailing towards Port Antonio and take the necessary defensive action.

It was here that Coward made his home which is surprisingly Spartan, particularly as he entertained lavishly, his guests including the Queen Mother and a host of other celebrities of the time.

Here, too, he is buried. A marble slab marks his burial site and nearby, as a memorial, is a statue of Noel Coward sitting on a garden seat looking thoughtfully out to sea designed and created by Angela Connor.

It is now a museum.

It is easy to see why Henry Morgan, Noel Coward and Ian Fleming chose this part of Jamaica in which to settle. Backed by the Blue Mountains and overlooking the Caribbean, the countryside is rich with forests, hillside plantations, valleys, waterfalls and it is cooled by the off-land winds in the evening known as the Undertaker's wind and freshened by the winds in the morning known as the Doctor's wind. It must have seemed as close to paradise as these men could get.

Passing this area, we arrived at Port Antonio with its twin harbours of west and east harbour protected by Navy Island at their entrances. At the centre of town was the Trident hotel but we turned inland and climbed up the hill to the Buonavista hotel guarded by an old cannon and a triangle of cannon balls that overlooked the town.

Port Antonio was far less developed than the towns like Montego Bay and Ocho Rios but became famous through the antics of a famous swashbuckling film star of the 1940s – Errol Flynn.

The story goes that, due to a storm, he had to moor his yacht in Kingston, the island's capital, on the south coast. He hired a motorcycle and drove round the east coast until he reached Port Antonio. He fell in love with it exclaiming that it was more beautiful than any woman he had ever known (and he was famous for knowing many).

Flynn decided to make a hedonistic home above the town so he purchased a 2000-acre ranch and the Titchfield hotel and began to entertain the rich and famous. One of Flynn's more interesting purchases (the locals claim that he won it in a rum fuelled poker game) was the 64-acres of Navy Island, the guardian of the harbours. Other than a hut on which lived the caretaker known as 'Governor', the island was uninhabited. Flynn would sail his friends over in his yacht for wild parties that increased his reputation as a hedonistic libertine.

After his death, various attempts were made to create a tourist destination on the island but none were successful and the island is again uninhabited and owned by the Government.

Errol Flynn's grandson, now owns the Titchfield estate and is in the process of developing it.

Errol Flynn's other claim to fame as far as Jamaica is concerned is that he is held responsible for popularizing one of Port Antonio's most famous attractions which is rafting down Jamaica's longest river, the Rio Grande.

The rafts are made from bamboo poles cut from the groves higher up in the hills and are 4 foot wide and 25 to 30 foot long. They are poled by the local rafters who pole from the front. Two passengers sit on an elevated 'love seat' which is placed across the raft further to the rear. Originally, they were used by farmers to carry bananas from their plantations higher up in the hills down to the harbour. Perhaps, they still are.

One thing Jamaicans know how to do well is to party – be it at home, at a venue, on a boat, or best of all, at picnics.

We drove up, again in convoy, to the start point to find our hosts had ordered eight rafts, four for us and four for the staff and our picnic supplies. These included red Stripe beer, Rum punches, Bullshots to slake our thirst and a voluptuous selection of picnic food to satisfy our hunger.

The view towards the Caribbean at Discovery Bay

The journey down usually takes two to three hours. We took five hours that included stops for refreshments (quite frequently), swimming and, in my case, an introduction to a strange cigarette called a spliff.

This marvellous trip to an area known as Jamaica's Riviera was over all too soon and we returned in convoy to Worthy Park for the few days left to us before our flight back to England.

What an incredible and memorable experience! Not only had I been introduced to the beauty of the island but also, I had met an exceptionally hospitable group of people – people who truly lived by the expression 'work hard and play hard'. I wondered if I would ever return or see them again.

It was time to return to England having enjoyed an extraordinary and memorable holiday. The whole experience, the people, the climate, the hospitality and the topography reminded me of my golden years in Hong Kong. I realised just how much of a Colonial I really was.

In this glow of gratitude and under the grey skies of England, I asked Hope if she would marry me. She consented and we became engaged.

'I think I first realised that I was perhaps not doing the right thing occurred when I was asked to prepare a guest list for the wedding. I asked if I could see theirs. The Archbishop of Canterbury was to officiate at the wedding ceremony; the guest list included the Prime Minister, most of the Tory cabinet and a host of other guests from the Masons and the world of finance.

My guest list included my parents, John and Kerrie Perridge, three couples from my university days, the odd old school friend and my two flat mates.

Then I began to be put under pressure to consider joining the Masons, to consider entering Tory central office and generally to move out of my comfort zone into a world that might be advantageous but would not make me happy. Three weeks before the wedding and with Lady Leather's understanding, I asked to see Hope in the London flat and told her I could not go on with the wedding. She threw my ring back at me and, quite rightly, told me to get out of her flat.

This was a Friday night so the next day I drove down to Folkestone to confirm to my parents the news. I arrived at just the wrong time as my father would be watching the racing. Much to my surprise, he was standing at the front door as I arrived. He came over to me, grasped my hand and exclaimed, "Ten years off my life, old boy. Your mother is having the odd tear or two but I assure you it is all for the best. Come in, the racing is on and then we will have lunch."

The oddest thing about the whole break up is that I assumed that I would never see the McConnells again and that my holiday in Jamaica would be an unforgettable memory and one that, naturally, I held with gratitude to Hope for whom I had a terrible feeling of guilt.

Time to move on. Time to get on with life.

One evening, a month or so later, Barry invited me to join him at one of his friend's party in Earl's Court. I was ambling around knowing nobody when I heard a Jamaican accent coming from a room down the hall. I went to investigate and introduced myself to a young woman who, it turned out, had been brought up in Jamaica. Her father was a doctor at a Tate and Lyle sugar estate in the furthest wilds of Jamaica in a town called Savannah-la-Mar (known island wide as Sav-la-Mar) on the southwest coast. She had come over to England to start nursing and was presently working on the Accident and Emergency ward at Charing Cross hospital.

Our conversation just flowed and I found that she vaguely knew of the McConnells as she had won a golf championship at their golf course at Worthy Park. Her friends were far more inclined to be from those near her home in her local area called Paradise near Sav-la-Mar. Incidentally, it was where a section of the movie Papillon was filmed.

She was planning to return to Jamaica for her summer holiday and asked whether I would like to join her. I was hardly likely to refuse.

We flew into Montego Bay to be met by Jane's parents who drove us from Montego Bay southwards over the mountains to the plains of Sav-la-Mar. Despite the luxuriant cane fields, this was quite a different Jamaica to the one I had become accustomed to. This was a low land area dominated by sugar cane, the plantation called Frome being owned by Tate and Lyle. Other than the cane, this was scrubland, better suited to cattle and smallholdings. The town of Sav-la-Mar did not have much going for it – just one main street, a church, a few shops and a town hall.

The town's heyday had been during the late 18th century when it had been a major port for the importation of slaves and general goods and the export of sugar. It did, however, have a remarkable claim to respect after the abolishment of slavery by the British in 1833, slavery remaining legal in the United States. Any ship docking at the port was boarded and freedom offered to any slaves who wished to stay in Jamaica. Over 200 slaves were freed by the British in this way.

The campus was very much like the ones I have seen before except that a nine-hole golf course ran through the centre of the houses – very convenient for a round before enjoying cocktails and dinner. Jane's parents were a delightful couple. Her father was the campus doctor whose antecedents had also been in the medical profession in Jamaica. He was English to the core and had served with the commandos during the war. Her mother had been born in India and was the live wire of the house, always looking for her pink gins which she would put down somewhere but couldn't remember where. They were to be found in linen cupboards, in the kitchen, in bedrooms and were a source of pleasure to me to count the number of different places they could be found in any one day.

Tommy, her father, explained that not only was he a doctor for the campus but also served the local population as well. He told me two delightful stories that have remained in my memory. The first was when he was attending a local woman who was pregnant with her eighth child. He asked if the children were from the same father. Her reply was, "Lord have mercy, doctor. If you are a pin cushion, how you know which pin prick you." Obviously, not monogamous.

The second story he told me was that, when he first arrived to take up his post, he realised that the local witch doctor or Obeah man was keeping those who really needed modern medical attention away from his surgery.

He decided he had to take on the Obeah man to prove that his magic was stronger than his adversary's. He arranged for the Obeah man to come to his surgery for a meeting. Tommy made up a concoction that he could lay on the walkway to his surgery which if trodden on would explode.

He carefully laid this on the walkway, commanding the Obeah man to enter through the back door so his presence would not be seen by the campus workers. After their meeting, Tommy told the Obeah man that his medical magic was so strong that when his adversary left by the front door, the ground would explode beneath his bare feet. He showed his adversary out through the front door.

I understand that the Obeah man is still running from the explosions beneath his feet and Tommy's surgery became open to all.

Jane at her wedding to Nick Ingram

The plantation had a seaside house in an area called Negril on the west coast and it was to this house we would go every weekend taking a picnic with us. The town of Negril, more a village than a town, included a tumbledown shop or two, a wooden shacked yacht club that had seen better days and a small hotel along the cliff face with rooms directly over the sea. It was an area filled by young hippies, mainly European and American who found delight in the locally grown weed as much as for the Red Stripe beer and the local rum.

The beauty of Negril was a seven-mile beach, totally unspoilt except for a few houses built on stilts dotted along the beachfront. In the right season, the crabs migrated from land to sea and there were thousands of them. The locals, including ourselves, would catch enough to enjoy with their barbecues or our picnics – picnics which if taken in the evening were made resplendent by the most beautiful sunsets in Jamaica.

It was an area that was later to become highly developed to meet a major push for mass tourism.

Our holiday flew by with a type of lotus eating life which allowed each day to merge pleasantly into the next. It did introduce me, however, to the might of tropical storms unknown to me from Hong Kong. My bedroom had a corrugated iron roof and it was after lunch in the early afternoon that it was the usual time both for an afternoon snooze and for the storms. Almost without warning, the sky would go black and the rain descend in torrents, drumming on my corrugated iron roof. Within twenty minutes, it was over and the sun shone brightly as if no storm had ever been.

It was quite magical, though I was once caught driving in a storm. The blackness was so thick that I could not see through the windscreen even with full head lights on. Time to be sensible and to pull in, have a cigarette and wait the short time until it cleared.

I returned to continue my life as a product manager of Gerber baby foods which now, at least, we distributed throughout the retail sector though continuing our battle for survival against Heinz.

One evening in the summer, I was at home when the phone rang. In his rich Jamaican accent, it was Peter McConnell who, obviously, I never expected to hear from again. His opening line was, "Hello Huntie, (my Jamaican nickname) how are you? Get your rass arse over here for some backgammon." I remonstrated that I thought I would never hear from him again. He enthused that there was no way they were going to lose their friendship with me and to come and join them. I did and we are still friends to this day.

I am not sure whether it was my natural charm and affability that was the reason for this continued friendship but I did have a slight suspicion that it was my membership to Annabel's that might also have been an attraction as this club became their second home whenever they were in London.

Amongst us product managers, there was a feeling that, at a certain point in our career, we should go to business school. Various of our colleagues had gone in the past two years to Cranfield Business School in the Midlands and the idea began to appeal to me, too.

I presented the idea to my parents who were so used to paying for my various shots at education that they decided that one more could do no harm. So, with their financial support and blessing, I took the entrance exam to join Cranfield for a year of business studies, passed their entrance exam so resigned from Gerber foods and set off for Cranfield in the Spring of 1969.

In 1964, as I have mentioned, the Conservative government had lost the election to the Labour Government led by Harold Wilson, famous for his ode to technology speech some years previously. This led to a belief by the unions that they could flex their muscles and it also led to a disastrous mismanagement of the economy.

There had been rumblings throughout the late 60s from the Unions in particular the Dockers and the Miners and it was in October 1969 that the Yorkshire Miners, approximately 70,000 of them led by Arthur Scargill of the National Union of Miners (NUM) went on unofficial strike. The strike lasted two weeks and introduced flying pickets where miners from one mine would picket other miners for not joining the strike.

Various improvements were introduced to the mining industry but, eventually they did not satisfy the strike minded miners led by Arthur Scargill which led to the Miners' strike which started in 1984 and lasted a year. Scargill had hoped that he would be able to organise a national strike by Unions but this never happened and eventually the Government of Margaret Thatcher broke the strike and dealt a blow to the strength of all the unions.

There were about 60 of us on the course at Cranfield, seriously weighted towards men. If memory serves, there was only one woman amongst us, Marylin. The college was divided between us the business students and the engineering students who probably outnumbered us by four to one. We amusingly referred to them, I don't quite know why, as Underwater Welders.

A view of part of the 5 mile beach at Negril

I soon found a small group of fellow students who thought that there was much to be learned on the course but it should not be taken without humour and some criticism. This caused me to create a small magazine, appropriately titled 'Funny Business' which took a scurrilous look at our lectures and lecturers and was produced at the end of each of our three terms. Some of my largest fans were the secretaries who typed and printed it. I understand that we were the only year ever to have produced such a light hearted critique of our studies and our lecturers that some took far too seriously.

This same group of students also realised that we would need some sort of hold over those who would mark our exam papers. We started a club called the Tuesday Club which had 10 members. The idea was that on two Tuesdays of each term, we would invite two lecturers out to dinner as our guests in a local restaurant. Much to our surprise, this became very popular amongst our lecturers and they jockeyed for an invitation.

There were some areas of the course that were quite beyond me. Advanced mathematics and flow charts for computer programmes to name just two. In one Mathematics class the lecturer started by saying that two plus two was only four with one degree of freedom. I was lost already.

Our accountancy lectures did, however, give me some respite. We had to deal with quite advanced accountancy subjects such as legal obligations, profit and loss accounts, balance sheets and the identity of hundreds of different costs. So much so that I wrote an article about costs which was considered amusing enough to be published in the Accountancy Magazine. I apologise for its student type naivety but I reproduce most of it here as it was my first piece of writing to be professionally published.

'It is definitely no fun being a Cost. I mean, if you're something else, at least you know what you are. You've got some sort of a group identity. But not us poor Costs. Nobody comes up to us. You'd feel a bit stupid saying, 'Good morning, Mr Discretionary Cost' or, 'Hello, Mrs Semi-annual Cost'. Well, you would, wouldn't you? You just don't think of our feelings. You just don't take any notice of us Costs.

'Mark you, to some degree it may be our fault. Old General Cost claims that the problem is social. We just don't have enough Class or Quality Costs.

'Nobody to talk to in the Cost Centre, he claims. Too many damned Common Costs. Too many Unavoidable Costs lolling about all over the place. Too many Impossible Costs with no deference for their betters. If he had his way, he'd be a Current Cost and electrocute the lot of them. But there's the real nub of the problem. Most of us are born Variable Costs. We just don't know what we are going to be from one minute to the next.

'I suppose I'm lucky, really. I'm a Fixed Overhead Cost. Gives me a detached point of view. But imagine the predicament of an Hourly Cost. In one day, he can have been netted, allocated, assigned, budgeted, deferred, engineered, estimated, imputed, managed, manufactured, maximised, minimised, materialised, absorbed, under-absorbed and over-absorbed, processed, prorated, set-up and set-down; and if he wasn't absorbed enough already, he could be semi-absorbed into the bargain. All this transfiguration isn't good for a fellow. It's no wonder that some Costs have split-personality problems. They just can't settle down to being Standard Costs.

'No, these days one has to specialise to get recognition. You have to be socially acceptable. You have to be a Prime Cost or a Relevant Cost or a well-balanced Discretionary Cost.

'We are doing the missionary work on our side. We've exterminated the Idle-Capacity Costs, streamlined the Gross Costs, operated on the Joint Costs, stepped on the Threshold Costs and avoided the Unavoidable Costs. So, we're not foot-dragging. But now we need your help at the Cost Centre. With the input of some rather attractive Extra Costs, we ask that you operate some Cost Cutting on most of us Costs and create an understandable language preferably in plain English that we can all understand.'

A third and strange activity was called, I think, a T group session. We were broken into small groups and for three days we were basically locked in a room with a psychiatrist. The idea, I believe, was to show us our basic animalistic nature. Oddly enough we did see, over the three days, how some people gang up on the weaker members and try to destroy them. It was actually quite unusual and, in some cases unnerving, but very interesting though I am not sure it had any effect on our later lives.

However, the intention of our training was to make us first managers and secondly entrepreneurs. The basis of this programme was to give us an overall view of business practices and the knowledge of where and how to find answers to problems that we might not have the background to solve.

An imposing part of the campus of Cranfield's
Institute of Technology

The practicality was that we had to go out and tackle our own consultancy projects, one after our first term and the second after our third and last term. This, our final consultancy project, counted as our thesis on which we were judged to be worthy (or not) of a degree as a Master of Business Administration.

I had difficulty finding anyone who might take me on as a consultant but, as luck would have it, I was dining one evening in the Poissonerie de l'Avenue restaurant in Sloane Avenue, one of my favourite restaurants and, in conversation with Peter Rossignoli, the owner, he said that he could help. He was interested in having an independent look at his business with an eye to expanding it.

With my background working in the Soup Bowl in Dublin, I might be perfect for the job. My problem was solved and as a result of my report, he acquired the next-door premises and expanded his restaurant. I am glad to say successfully.

My final consultancy project and my thesis dealt with some acquaintances who manufactured old pine furniture under the title, Designwoods Limited and also ran a retail outlet under the name Pinocchio Furniture Limited in Putney, West London. There is an old adage that most problems with companies stem from those that run or own them. This was very true in my case.

The two companies were separate but joined by agreements and, originally, by friendship. However, the retail business was meant to generate sales for the manufacturing side but it never produced enough volume to justify the cost of manufacturing.

Neither company had assessed the market or had planned any strategy to reach it. The result was that the two companies were going in different directions with mutual recriminations and the threat of the dissolution of one or both companies. I was employed to try and sort out the mess.

It was an uphill struggle but I proposed that they should virtually start again with a new trading agreement.

Designwoods would continue to manufacture old pine furniture and Pinocchio Limited would act as its sales agent in the UK retail market. Designwoods would be free to manufacture furniture from any other woods and to market their products overseas or on a contract basis.

There were further agreements that foresaw the end of Pinocchio Limited and the total operation being marketed under the Designwoods Company name. However, this depended on a realignment of the directors' shares and the stated wish of the directors of Pinocchio to leave the furniture trade being realised.

Frankly, the original basis on which the companies were created was unworkable and was made by complete amateurs with no idea of what is required to run a business. The only proficient one was the designer and manufacturer of old pine furniture but he needed a competent manager to handle the business side of his design and products.

I was thanked and I was thankful to have completed my thesis. It had not been the happiest experience but I seemed to have pleased the directors and, more importantly, I had only the final exams to pass to achieve my professional qualification.

Amongst a year of considerable pressure, there were lighter moments. What I did enjoy was that I was introduced by the roommates next door to the music of Crosby, Stills and Nash and Simon and Garfunkel.

I was also introduced to the daughter of a farmer who lived nearby who was delightfully free with her concept of how to relax this poor hard-working student by spending the afternoons in his study.

Our weekends were free and so it was our normal practice to drive back down to our home in London for the weekends to join our regular girlfriends.

From time to time, Cranfield would invite a guest speaker to dinner that would be followed by an after-dinner speech. One memorable guest was Enock Powell, a right-wing politician famous for his opposition to immigration from the Caribbean in particular forecasting rivers of blood in the streets if too many immigrants were forced upon local communities.

He was a very forceful and entertaining speaker and, later, was to become a major critic of the Heath Government.

When the evening had ended, I set off, perhaps with the odd glass of wine more than I would normally have taken before an hour's drive, to be stopped by the police half-way back down the M1. "Good evening, sir, may I ask where you have been?"

"Oh, Officer," I replied, "I have just left Cranfield where we had dinner with Enock Powell."

"Wonderful man," came the Officer's reply. "If you see him again, tell him we are right behind him. Carry on, sir, and safe home." Nothing like a bit of prejudice to keep the wheels turning!

At the end of the summer term, we took our final exams. Somehow, I managed to keep my rate of only one failure at exams so far in my life.

I was now a Master of Business Administration or MBA, more initials to add to my MA (Trinity) and my MinstM (Marketing). However, I was now to collect another failure. And rather sooner than I expected.

Various head hunters approached us through the summer term to discover if we were interested in their wares. One, a consultancy firm in Knightsbridge, quite took my fancy so I applied and was called in for an interview on a Friday morning at 08.30 am.

On arrival, I was given an intelligence test to complete. I presented my best effort and was called into an office where a rather severe looking man began by asking me if I had actually completed the course at Cranfield. I said, yes, I had. How then, he asked me, did I have an IQ of 60, lower than even the lowest grade of cleaning staff in his offices?

I thought it best to come clean and explained that I had only left Annabel's at about 2 am to go on to Tramps until about 4 am and then had been kept quite busy by my girlfriend until I just had enough time to shave and dress for our interview. Despite my protestation that a consultancy firm should always have someone on their staff that was not cut from the same mould as everyone else, I was shown the door with some unsympathetic firmness.

I was, however, successful with an application to join a company called Cavenham Limited, owned by Jimmy Goldsmith who was, at this stage, setting out on his illustrious career to become a multi-millionaire. My appointment was as marketing manager for the Confectionary company which, at the time I joined, was losing £300,000 per year.

The confectionary company controlled three factories, one in Bristol which made a range of children's products under the name of Goodies, a line of liqueur chocolates called Famous Names and the very popular line of Elizabeth Shaw's mint crisps. The Parkinson factory in Doncaster made Parkinson's boiled sweets and the factory in Southport made

Chewits and toffees. I worked out one day that if you took every flavour and every product that we made, I had over 600 lines of confectionary to market.

My production manager in Bristol told me that we sold annually enough white mice, a sort of milky, sugary, palm oil product for children, that if they were placed end to end, they would travel round the moon and back. One of the lines that I never had time to concentrate on was a range of rather unattractive chewing gums from Italy. Every Friday evening, Jimmy Goldsmith would come into my office and which line did he always ask about? His damned Italian chewing gums.

The first hurdle we and everyone else had to surmount was the introduction of decimal currency scheduled for January 1971. Anyone born after 1971 would be surprised by the ease which we, of an elder generation, dealt with the system that had 12 pence to the shilling and 20 shillings to the pound.

Pre-decimal currency had been created in the reign of King Henry II (1133-1189) and had developed its own popular language. From lowest to highest, the currency began with a farthing (1/4 of a penny, a happence (1/2 a penny), a penny, a thruppence (three pence), a tanner (six pence), a shilling, a florin (2 shillings), a half-crown (2 shillings and 6 pence), a crown (5 shillings), a half sovereign (10 shillings), a sovereign or a pound, (20 shillings), a half guinea (10 shillings and sixpence), a guinea (£1 and 1 shilling).

One of the problems was in the lower price points, particularly for us as many of our children's products sold for an old penny and this did not convert directly. The lowest decimal coin was a half-penny which would mean an inflationary increase in our products. (In fact, the decimal half pence did not last more than a few years and the one penny coin became the lowest valued coin).

Often the only recourse we had was to reduce the weight of the product in order to maintain its profitability.

The media was full of forecasts of doom and gloom but the conversion day dawned and the new coinage was quickly accepted and the old coins either returned to the banks or saved by collectors.

The strange thing about living through the rest of the chaos of the 1970s is that we carried on living our lives coping on a daily basis. We began and continued to live through racial tension, hyperinflation combined with ever-increasing unemployment, numerous strikes, power cuts, three-day working weeks, mob violence, gang warfare and the bombing of civilian targets. Perhaps the critical price increase that influenced most of this hyperinflation was the price of crude oil.

Due to the Yom Kippur war between Egypt and Israel in 1973, the price of crude oil rose from $3 per barrel to $12 per barrel and later in 1979 to $39.50 per barrel. It is not surprising that Britain became known as 'the poor man of Europe'.

For those who might be interested, there were a lot of lows but some highs in this tempestuous decade. I have picked some of both, which to me reflect this extraordinary decade in British history.

1969

The year that the civil disturbances in Northern Island came to a head.

1970

Edward Heath (Conservative) becomes Prime Minister.

First 747 (Jumbo jet) aircraft flight by PanAm lands at Heathrow.

Age of majority reduced from 21 to 18.

18 victims of thalidomide awarded £320,000 in compensation.

English golfer Tony Jacklin wins US open.

Dockers go on strike generating a state of emergency.

British Petroleum discovers large oil field under the North Sea.

1971

The Conservative government introduces non-conciliatory policies in Ulster.

BBC Open University broadcasts begin.

Rolls Royce becomes bankrupt and taken over by the Government.

Hard Rock Café opens its first café near Hyde Park Corner.

CAT scan (invented by G. Hounsfield) used for the first time.

Ibrox disaster, 66 die and many injured in the Glasgow stadium.

Birmingham's spaghetti junction opened.

Unemployment reaches 815,000 – a post war high.

Chay Blyth completes his solo sail around the world from east to west.

Britain expels 90 Russian diplomats for spying.

Bomb exploded on the top of the Post Office tower.

1972

Bloody Sunday. The Parachute Regiment opened fire on Ulster civilians. 13 killed.

Strike led by Artur Scargill and the National Union of Miners (NUM). 24,000,000 working days lost.

BEA flight 548 crashes over Staines, 118 people killed.

Aldershot barracks bombed, six killed.

The murder of athletes at the Munich Olympics.

The dockers again go on strike. The three-day week initiated.

Second cod war begins after Icelandic gunboats sink two British trawlers.

Thousands of Ugandan-Asians were given sanctuary after being expelled by Idi Amin.

Cambridge colleges admit female undergraduates.

1973

Firebombs placed in Harrods – a warning given each time.

Arab-Israeli war.

Britain, Ireland and Denmark join the Common market. For Britain, this was the third attempt, the previous ones have been vetoed by General de Gaulle of France.

British share values fall by £4,000,000,000 in one day.

Women admitted to the London Stock Exchange.

1.6 million workers go on strike over pay restraints.

Markham colliery disaster in which 18 miners lost their lives.

Dalai Lama visits the UK for the first time.

The Sunningdale agreement signed which was intended to bring about power sharing in Northern Island. The agreement lasted until May of the following year.

1974

Harold Wilson (Labour) becomes Prime Minister.

Further general election towards the end of the year, also won by Harold Wilson.

Civilians murdered by the IRA notably in Birmingham and Guildford. Bombings continue including Tower of London, Houses of Parliament, even the Prime Minister's home.

Rail workers and civil servants go on strike.

Value added tax (VAT) introduced.

ABBA win Eurovision song contest with 'Waterloo'.

Oxford University admits women for the first time.

Lord Lucan disappears.

McDonalds opens its first restaurant in the UK.

Princess Royal marries Mark Phillips in Westminster Abbey.

China gives gift of two giant pandas, Ching-Ching and Chia-Chia, to London Zoo.

1975

North Sea oil pipeline to UK opened.

Strikes cause the loss of 15,000,000 working days.

Inflation approaches 30%.

Watergate scandal – three of Nixon's aides imprisoned.

British Leyland taken under government control.

London Hilton bombed, two killed, 63 injured.

Spaghetti house siege.

Vietnam War ended – unconditional surrender of South Vietnam.

1976

Jim Callaghan (Labour) becomes Prime Minister after Wilson resigns.

Hurricane force winds blow up to 105 mph killing 22 and causing massive damage.

Concorde takes first commercial flight from London to Bahrain.

National Exhibition Centre in Birmingham opened by the Queen.

UK wins European Song Contest with Brotherhood of Man's 'Save your kisses for me'.

UK and Iceland negotiate an end to the cod war.

Intercity 125 train enters service between Paddington and the west.

Endless summer: 22 days with temperatures in the 90s.

James Hunt becomes Formula One World champion.

1977

Queen's Silver Jubilee.

UK holds presidency of the Council of the European Union for the first time.

Riots at Notting Hill Carnival, 100 people injured.

Firefighters go on strike for nine-weeks and Undertakers leave 800 corpses unburied.

Media including BBC blacked out.

North Sea oil begins production.

M5 is completed, 15 years after it was first started.

Red Rum wins the Grand National for the third time.

Marches by the National Front (Far Right) cause rioting in Lewisham and Birmingham.

Skytrain launched by Freddy Laker from Gatwick to New York.

BA launches regular supersonic fights between London and New York.

Introduction of Punk music.

1978

BBC shut down for days before Christmas.

Times newspaper, due to strikes, is closed for a year.

11 killed in Taunton train fire.

23 Ford plants closed due to strikes.

The State's earnings-related pension scheme introduced.

Anna Ford appointed by ITN, the first female newsreader on TV.

12 people killed in Le Bon restaurant bombing.

William Stern declared bankrupt with debts of £118 million.

Naomi James becomes the first woman to sail single handed around the world.

Bakers go on strike.

Pound sterling recovering and balance of trade stronger – a portent for happier times.

However, industrial conflict continues.

1979

Severe weather conditions throughout winter of 1978/1979.

Tens of thousands of workers go on strike in what becomes known as 'the winter of discontent'.

Strikes cause 30,000,000 working days lost.

1000 schools close.

London's Jubilee line opened.

Margaret Thatcher (Conservative) becomes Prime Minister.

Airey Neave in London and Lord Mountbatten of Burma in Eire are assassinated by the IRA.

The sale of nationalised industries begins.

Airport screening introduced.

Brighton opens first beach for naturalists.

Fastnet yacht race hit by storms in the Irish Sea, 15 lives and dozens of yachts are lost.

Milton Keynes' indoor shopping centre is opened – the largest in Britain.

All foreign travel restrictions are lifted. Council tenants are given the right to purchase their council houses. Five million tenants occupy council property.

I have gone on about the 1970s in some detail because it was the most extraordinary decade that I have lived through due, in particular, for the constant threat of terrorist bombing and the innumerable strikes. However, not only does life go on but there were opportunities for wealth to be taken and important social improvements.

Asset stripping is the practice of taking over a company in financial difficulties (or which is just being badly managed) in order to break up the company and sell off its assets separately at a profit with no regard to the company's future or the extant labour force. Jim Slater and his partner Peter Walker were the most famous of the asset strippers but there were many who jumped on the band wagon including my boss Jimmy Goldsmith.

The City of London was not far behind in realising the potential for new methods of making money.

It became far more aware of trading and dealing outside the traditional way with the development of merchant banks, venture capitalists and off the wall Ponzi promoters who were not necessarily bound by any moral limitations. Their only objective was to make money.

Born in the 1960s, the recognition of women as equal citizens improved by leaps and bounds. Universities and traditional businesses became open to women of talent and helped develop a new world of women's self-expression.

Through the welfare system and with increased benefits, wealth was slowly being more evenly distributed through the levels of society and a realisation that government had responsibilities for others than just the rich.

The seeds were also sown from the mid-1970s for the devolution of power to the Scottish, Welsh and Northern Irish communities who traditionally had been managed by the English parliament. Eventually, they were all to receive their own seats of local power and influence.

Britain continued to be as creative as ever. The Beatles and the Rolling Stones, David Bowie, Elton John, Gary Glitter and the Punk rockers such as the Sex Pistols and the Clash led the music charts not just at home but in large overseas markets.

In my personal life, my girlfriend and I parted company. It seems that after each major career move, I gain employment but lose a girlfriend. I am sure it can have nothing to do from not necessarily being completely monogamous but surely not. I entered a period of having girlfriends rather than a girlfriend, one of whom, Margaret, a Jamaican girl living in London, was to have a dramatic influence on my future life.

I entered with enthusiasm into my career, marketing our confectionary products and as a team, after a year, we had managed to bring the company into profitability which continued to grow. We believed that it was this reversal in Goldsmith's fortunes that put him in a position to plan a take-over of Bovril and, then, on to the development of his food empire.

One of my girlfriends Kay, a South African, had decided to leave London and return home to Cape Town. She invited me to join her on one of my holidays. I flew down first to Johannesburg to stay for a couple of nights with friends who had been colleagues at Cranfield. I found the city scary as the atmosphere appeared to be slightly hostile with houses grilled and protected by well-armed security forces. Not very appealing.

Cape Town was quite a different matter.

After an invigorating re-union, Kay presented me with a touring itinerary for the two of us that included visiting the Eastern Cape, Port Elizabeth, the Garden Route and wineries at Stellenbosch. After this, we were to travel north toward Kimberley and finally, after a brief visit to Pretoria, a coach trip to the Kruger Park for a three-day safari. She did not hold back on giving me the full introduction to just a tiny part of South Africa during my three weeks' visit.

What struck me most on our trips towards the north was the vastness of the country. Coming from a small island, I actually found this rather overwhelming. As we drove north the scenery did not seem to change at all. It took some getting used to – the magnificence and incredible space of it – so unbelievably different to the immediate variety of the English countryside.

However, one of the local characteristics that I enjoyed most was eating in restaurants because, despite excellent food, they did not have our equivalent of liquor licenses. You brought your own wine allowing you to choose from your own selection and without a heavy profit mark-up. Barbecues, of course, were mandatory.

I also enjoyed wonderful summer weather which I was told was one of the joys of living on the Cape as well as appreciating the majesty of Table Mountain and the stunning scenery particularly to the east of this meeting point between two of the world's great oceans.

It was when we were entering the Kruger Park in our coach for a three-day visit that I was introduced to the quirkiness of South African humour. The coach had to cross a railway line at the entrance to the park and, as we crossed the lines, the driver/guide called out to us, "Look ladies and gentlemen, lions." Then, the necessary pause followed by, "Railway lions". I thought three days of this humour might be unbearable but, thank goodness, he left us to enjoy seeing the full splendour of both the flora and fauna and all the wild life (including lions) that you could wish to see on a first visit.

Having said this, I have to admit I thoroughly enjoyed my holiday but it gave me no immediate desire to return despite the charms of my girlfriend with whom I have stayed in touch annually since those days. However, it was now time for me to return.

On my return, I began to be called into Jimmy's office quite often and given projects to do for him. The first was to be sent to our factory in Doncaster to tell them that the factory was to be closed and the products transferred to Bristol.

Somehow, this news leaked and I was met at the station by a hostile crowd of employees waving banners and physically threatening me. I had to be escorted by police to a waiting car. This same hostility met me on my return to the station. In the event, Jimmy backed down and the factory remained open.

It was after I was asked to create and prepare some twenty gift packages to be given to a selection of financial journalists that Jimmy had invited in for a presentation that I went to my managing director to ask what was going on.

He explained to me that Jimmy was considering moving me into his domain and appointing a new person to take over confectionary. I had not been consulted about this and I replied that I did not want to mess about on footling projects and that I enjoyed my position marketing confectionary. However, it seemed that this is what was planned and what was going to happen. I was not amused.

Fate again took a hand.

Margaret, my Jamaican friend, telephoned me to say that a marketing job was being offered by the Jamaican Government and would I be interested. She thought it would suit me down to the ground. The requirement was for someone who would market Jamaican products that would be viable to sell in the UK and Europe. I couldn't imagine anything I would like more so I applied and was accepted.

I left Cavenham and moved into my new office positioned on the first floor of the Jamaican High Commission in Mayfair. Our official title was 'Jamco, the trade organisation of the Government of Jamaica'. The operation had been set up by our Chairman, John Pringle, one of the leading promoters of Jamaica. He was an enthusiastic member of a small group that were responsible for the development of Jamaica as a major tourist destination.

The managing director was Arthur Jefferes, a northern Irish man who had been at Trinity, Dublin some years before me and his assistant, Neville. We were three white men in the heart of London's Jamaica.

I have always enjoyed Jamaican humour and it delighted me no end to find that we were referred to by the Commission staff as 'Little Rhodesia'.

Jamaica had three major export products bauxite, the raw material of aluminium, sugar managed basically by Tate and Lyle and bananas handled by Arthur and Neville. My responsibility was the rest and my first priority would be to develop the UK and European market for Jamaican handmade cigars, a market dominated by Cuba.

There were three cigar manufacturers, all based around the capital city, Kingston, one of which was owned by an American company in New York. Correspondingly, there were three British importer/distributors, all based in London. Each distributor had the rights to specific Cuban cigar brands which were the bulk of their sales and the backbone of their profitability. Sales of Jamaican cigars became a very small second.

A cigar is made of two parts, the inner part known as the filler and the outer part known as the wrapper. It is generally accepted that some 80% of the flavour comes from the wrapper, the filler giving bulk but also defining the final smoking balance. Cuba has had, for centuries, the perfect soil and climate to produce the finest leaves for wrappers. Oddly enough, when I first learnt about cigars, I was told by those in the know that the finest cigars ever produced were just after the war. There was an embargo on Havana cigars so the wrappers were secretly sold to Jamaica and the cigar produced had the filler from Jamaica and the wrapper from Cuba. Once the embargo was lifted, this happenstance was sadly never repeated and this historic cigar never again produced.

My terms of employment were not as generous as they had been at Cavenham but they did include an annual trip to Jamaica via the American company in New York to present my report on the past year and the marketing plans for the following one. If needed, other trips might be necessary. As befitted a civil servant, these trips were generously accommodated in first-class on Air Jamaica or British Airways. I invariably managed to add on two weeks of my holiday allocation to visit my Jamaican friends and extend my social circle amongst their family.

It was on one of my early holiday visits that I was asked by Faye, Joan and her sister, Sheila, and later by her cousin, Diana, if I would be guardian to their children who were being sent to school in England. As they had 14 children between them, though not all of them were sent to England, some were educated in Canada, I had a delightful time looking after them when needed and, particularly with the girls, as, through them, I began to understand a little more about women than my normal experience had allowed.

It might be time to give my readers a little picture of the Jamaica that I experienced during the 1970s and early 1980s.

The name Jamaica means land of wood and water and the island is lush with forests, green valleys and plains, flowing rivers and attractive waterfalls set against the backdrop of the mountains. The island is about 150 miles by 50 miles and the mountain ranges run along the spine virtually from east to west. The south is the more mercantile side of the island and the home of Kingston, the capital.

The north is the land for tourism running from Negril in the west along the coast via Montego Bay and Ocho Rios to Port Antonio in the east. In boom times, the island welcomes around 4.3 million tourists per year.

Around the mountains, in the valleys and the plains, wherever it was viable to plant, the farmers, large and small, planted sugar cane, bananas, coconuts, vegetables and in the Blue Mountains, coffee. The climate was perfect for growth, being a combination of rain and sunshine though, always in the season, with the threat of hurricanes.

The country gained its independence from Britain in 1962. The island enjoyed a period of economic growth after independence but the wealth was not evenly distributed and left a class of urban poor concentrated in crime ridden shanty towns mainly to the west of Kingston.

In 1970, the population was 1.8 million which had increased to 2.1 million by 1982, a reasonably undramatic growth compared to other, like for like, developing countries.

The Queen, the hereditary monarch, is represented in Jamaica by a governor-general, the de facto head of state. During my time, the governor-general had the delightful name of Sir Florizel Augustus Glasspole, ON, GCMG, GCVO, CD who had had a very productive political life and then served Jamaica with distinction as Governor General from 1973 until 1991.

Politically, Jamaica's voters are represented by two parties – the Jamaican Labour party (JLP) and the People's National Party (PNP). The JLP representing the central right, the PNP the left.

I was to see a dramatic change during my tenure at Jamco when the JLP, supported by America, lost the election in 1972 to Michael Manley and his PNP party. Michael Manley introduced his democratic socialist programme which had merits but he lost the support of America and turned for friendship to Cuba.

Michael Manley was a man of great personal charm and vitality. He had that charisma that makes a person to whom he is speaking feel that he or she is the only person of interest to him while they are talking. He even bothered on occasion to cast his spell on this lowly civil servant when we met at some function.

His political agenda included free education, equal pay for women, land reforms to provide the tens of thousands of small farmers with land and credit, free healthcare and the automatic recognition of unions.

However, his programme also included verbal attacks on Americans and Europeans who had invested in homes in Jamaica as well as Jamaican landowners and entrepreneurs which resulted in many families deciding to split up with some members keeping their businesses going and others making a life in America or Canada.

Violence which had become endemic during the early 1970s, fuelled by drug money, as Jamaica was not only one of the world's largest producers of marijuana but was also, perhaps not fortuitously, positioned as a half-way house between America and the cocaine and heroin producers of South America.

Manley's government faced not only the effects of this violence but suffered from the loss in income from tourism, from the departure of entrepreneurs and from the support of America. Particularly in the larger towns, you made sure that you did not put yourself at risk by avoiding various areas of each town, traveling with your doors locked and stayed in houses that were grilled and barred.

It was not a happy time but for me, I had the consolation of spending my weekends when working in Kingston at Worthy Park.

The Worthy Park Sugar Estate is set in a beautiful valley called Lluidas Vale and is managed by my good friend, Peter McConnell. To reach it, I would drive out from Kingston along the coast to Spanish Town where I turned north to climb up the river road through Bog Walk, through Linstead (home of the famous market) and on to Ewarton at the base of Mount Diablo. Here, I would bear left and climb further up into the mountains to reach a point where I could look out and over the whole estate of Worthy Park – a patchwork of greens from the sugarcane fields and the surrounding hillsides and drive down into the valley to be greeted by their ever-delightful Jamaican hospitality.

It really was like a haven of peace away from the pressure of keeping safe in Kingston in particular. I could understand why everyone I knew carried a gun. I was offered one but I thought one of two disastrous things would happen if I carried one. I would either shoot myself in my foot or the villain would see the gun which would give him a reason to take it from me – probably rather violently. I did, however carry a machete in the car just for my own satisfaction rather than having any thought that I might actually use it.

A view of Worthy Park from a painting taken from the road into the estate

Peter and Joan had a beautiful bull mastiff dog called Jason. Jason and I were great friends and according to my hosts, I was the only person the dog would obey. When they wanted Jason to do his male stuff, they could get nowhere with him. When I said to Jason, "Jason, you go for it", he would centre his eyes on his intended mate, shrug his broad shoulders, give himself a shake and march up and onto his momentary bride.

Black country farmers do not like dogs. A few miles beyond the valley of Worthy Park near a town called Moneague, up in the bush was a wonderful jerk pork shack – as good as any in Jamaica and if I was at a loose end, I would take Jason up there with me.

He would usually sleep in the back of the car for the journey. When I parked near the shack, it was not unusual for a group of Jamaican farmers who just sort of appeared from the bush to surround the car. They were in no way aggressive. It was just curiosity to see what on earth a white man was doing out in the bush far from anywhere. It was at this moment that Jason would raise to his full height on the back seat. With shrieks of, "Lord, have mercy, big dog", they were gone and Jason and I would ascend to the shack in peace and quiet to purchase jerk pork and chicken and a couple of jerk sausages for Jason as his reward – happy man and happy dog that day.

Despite this confusion, the country continued to function bolstered by the resilience of those that stayed to run their businesses and from the recognition of the island in sport and, in particular, from the popularisation of Reggae, Jamaica's creative music, made world-famous by Bob Marley and the Wailers.

And so, back to England and my life as a Jamaican civil servant.

One of the first things I knew I had to do was to convince the importer/distributors that I was working for the interests of Jamaica but it would also be in their interest as well to increase their sales by working with me. I managed to convince them to supply me their monthly sales figures on the understanding that I would not divulge this information to their competitors.

I, therefore, created a basis of sales on which to work. My best-selling cigar brand was Royal Jamaica, manufactured by the Gore family who became great friends, in particular, Robert, who, with his uncle, ran their tobacco plantation and their factory.

It was through them that I learnt a very important lesson as a consultant. They had asked me to study the working practices of their labour force of cigar makers – those that rolled the cigars by hand to see how their productivity could be increased.

I suggested an incentive scheme to increase production. The effect was immediate and for the first four days of the week, the production soared. However, no one turned up on the Friday. It was explained to me by the work force that they were quite happy with the amount they had earned in four days so why turn up on the fifth. Life was too short and there were the pleasures of life outside the factory to enjoy once they had earned the amount they required for the week. Lesson learnt – know all about the requirements of your workers before interfering.

On one of their visits to London, Robert Gore and his uncle invited me out to one particular lunch. We had a seriously enjoyable and long well-oiled meal at which the idea arose to create a record promoting Royal Jamaica – a popular method at that time of promoting products. I was given the task of arranging it.

Through contacts in the Jamaican High Commission, I was introduced to Ezeke Grey, a reggae musician and singer who worked with and at a recording studio called Trojan records in Kensal Rise in West London.

This was a year in West Indian Test cricket history when, I think for the first time, their team won a test series of five matches against an old rival, the Australians.

We decided to make the record with the A side, a song to celebrate this famous victory – the first line of which was 'It was a day of jubilation when the West Indies beat the Australians' and continued to praise the players and their feats. The B side was a song praising the delights of smoking Royal Jamaica cigars.

The Gores were very happy with it, Ezeke was very happy with it, I was very happy with it but I have to admit it never raised any enthusiasm with the record buying public.

A by-product of this adventure was that I was asked by the recording studios if I could produce any lyrics that their musicians could use. I did prepare quite a few lyrics, a few lines of two of them, I remember. The first included the immortal lines:-

"Down a Trench Town, me get no work
Women wailing, Picknie die
Think of good times, times gone by."

And the second:-

"Do you remember the days of slavery?
"And the peoples and the times so hard."

I now have to admit that they got no further than our Royal Jamaica record.

Incidentally, it always amused me to be told the minute someone knew that I was involved with cigars that hand-made Havana and Jamaican cigars were rolled on the exposed thighs of handsome women. The fact is that only men rolled cigars up to the second world war.

I am convinced that this misrepresentation was based on the cigarillo factories of Spain during the nineteenth century. The story goes that the young female factory workers were often visited by the young men about town looking for an attractive girl to take out. The girls were also looking for some man who might take their fancy. The factories were so hot that the girls worked topless. So, to attract their man, they would raise their skirts and roll the cigarillos on their thighs.

True or not, it does make more sense.

Working within the cigar industry, it was necessary to concentrate on a very small and particular world. In England, as I have said, there were three distributors.

In France, there was only one – Monsieur Dufore who lived in splendour in the sixth arrondissement – the elite part of Paris. As the whole tobacco industry is controlled by the government, Monsieur Dufore was a friend of the President and it seemed to me also to the whole cabinet as well as their wives. Invariably, a large selection of them attended the evening parties to which he kindly invited me when I was visiting.

I felt honoured to be included and to meet, if even briefly, some of the elegant men and women who were the hierarchy of the French establishment. I am also glad that they were so well-mannered that they realised that my French was fifth-form kindergarten so spoke to me in English. It was greatly appreciated.

One of the perks of my employment was that I dealt with the duty-free trade, which every five years would hold a grand meeting at a chosen venue. I attended one in Amsterdam where we were privileged to enjoy a private visit to the Van Gogh museum followed by a dinner in its great hall, specially arranged for our evening.

Journalist, actor, aviator and bon viveur, Peter Geoffrey Holt Tory

From my Cavenham days, when I managed my 600 lines, one range I marketed was Famous Names liqueur chocolates. I knew a handful of delegates from this other small world – that of the liqueur importers. You may imagine we were a merry gang and could not resist the post dinner tour of Amsterdam's famous red-light district. I have to admit that once seen soon forgotten but it did, at least, put seedy Soho into the shade.

My almost regular girlfriend was a dizzy, young lady called Val. She insisted that I should meet a great friend of hers, another Peter, with those dreaded words, "I am sure you will really like each other".

She arranged for us to meet Peter and his girlfriend Gwen at a restaurant in Putney called the Wild Thyme. There is no doubt that we both shared the feeling that this meeting might be a disaster so had a few drinks before the meeting. Peter worked for the Daily Express, had been a RADA trained actor, a member of the Royal Shakespearian Company and was a fascinating and an interesting companion. I don't know how we got onto the subject of flying but Peter was an enthusiastic private pilot and I had dabbled with a few lessons in a Cessna, twice in Jamaica and twice in Jersey.

One of my exceptional memories from one of my flying lessons in Jamaica was being introduced to a manoeuvre that involved stalling the aircraft so that it spun out of control from 3000 feet down towards the approaching ocean. This took place over the sea in the bay of Kingston. It was truly magnificent experience because, as we spun, I was immersed in the view of the bay, the town and the Blue Mountains revolving around me – a vista of sea, town and mountains that could not be replicated in many places on earth. Just incredible!

However, we were a merry group and did not hold back on the number of bottles of wine we ordered. One of the few things I did remember other than agreeing with Val that Peter and his girlfriend were delightful company was that we had decided that we would buy an airplane and I would learn to fly in it.

The next morning, nursing a hangover in my office, I remembered this agreement and thought how could I get out of it. Why on earth had I agreed with someone I hardly knew that I would buy half an aircraft with him? Hopefully, he would have forgotten all about it.

It must have been about 11 am when the phone rang and it was Peter at his most cheerful. Obviously, he did not suffer from hangovers.

"Peter," he began, "good news. I think I have found an aircraft that would be perfect for us." Oh dear, how could I get out of this?

"Peter," I replied, "excellent news but (a brilliant excuse struck me) but I can only afford about £1000. That would be my limit." I was quite sure that this would be the perfect excuse and I could withdraw with honour.

His reply was immediate.

"That couldn't be better. I have found a Chipmunk that would be perfect for both of us. It is an ex-RAF trainer and fully aerobatic. It is absolutely perfect for you to learn on and for me to practice my stalls and turns not to mention the fun of flying a tail dragger (whatever that may mean). It is on the market for just under £2000 and with an extra £200 we can get a second inhibited Gypsy Major engine to replace the present one when it runs out – probably not for ten years yet. I can't tell you how exciting this is and I am sure we will have years of fun with it."

What could I say but wonderful? I was about to be the proud owner of a 'tail dragger' called a Chipmunk, an aircraft

I had never heard about and in partnership with a man whom I had only just met for the first time the night before.

Hey ho. Another chapter for good or bad was about to begin.

I first met the aircraft, registration G-BCRX, nicknamed by Peter, 'Myfanwy' (why, I never found out) at a small aerodrome to the north west of London called Denham. It had a west/east grass runway, office huts and a flying school to the south and hangers and huts to the north. We were lucky enough to rent a hut which included a table, two chairs and a filing cabinet in which we could keep our log books, headsets and flying maps and instructions.

De Havilland had developed the Chipmunk as a mono winged trainer for pilots who had previously been trained on the Tiger Moth bi-plane as the then modern fighters such as the Hurricane and Spitfire were mono winged aircraft.

Like the fighters that the RAF trainees were going to fly, the Chipmunk had its steering wheel at the back of the aircraft so when sitting in the aircraft you looked upward and going forward had to swerve the aircraft from side to side in order to see over the nose. (The reason they were called tail draggers).

On the runway, once you had lined up, you applied the power, held the aircraft straight until you had enough speed to raise the tail and, as the speed increased, pull the stick back until the aircraft became airborne and you were on your way.

The cockpit could not have been simpler. In front of you was your instrument panel with dials that measured speed, height and direction.

To your left, you had the throttle and to the right, the lever for the flaps – up, down and half way. Below the instrument panel was the radio and between it and you the joystick, push forward to descend, pull back to rise, push left to go left and right to go right.

Finally, at your feet were two pedals, left and right, to control the rudder and when pushed forward controlled the brakes. The rudder controlled your left and right movement on the ground and balanced the aircraft when you turned in the air. Your fuel tanks were on your wings with a dial showing the amount of fuel in your tanks – enough when full for about 200 miles flying at our cruising speed of just over 100 miles per hour.

Having been introduced to the aircraft, I was introduced by Peter to the man who was to be my instructor – Brian Lecomber.

G-BCRX - our Chipmunk aircraft on which I learnt to fly

Brian was an extraordinary character. He had flown for the Rothman aerobatic team, was a solo aerobatic pilot during the summer air show season, wrote thrillers, constantly smoked a pipe and used his Swan Vestas match box to explain aerobatic manoeuvres. He was dedicated to flying and enthusiastic about teaching people to fly and to share his obvious passion.

One of the books he wrote was entitled 'Talk Down', a story about a passenger in a small aircraft being talked down by air traffic control after the pilot became unconscious. It featured our call sign, G-BCRX and was later filmed to show that a talk down to a passenger is possible.

There are two parts to learning to fly. The first is the actual control of the aircraft which included a disciplined approach not only to attention whilst flying but also understanding where you were in the sky particularly, as we did, turn ourselves upside down and round and round, sometimes experiencing quite a strong force of gravity or g force.

The second is the paper work and the method of communicating by radio with air traffic control. This involves map reading and aviation law, subjects on which you have to take and pass a written examination.

It always amused me that we had to know that, if we suddenly saw puffs of black and white smoke bursting in front of us, it was to advise us that we were approaching a restricted military area. I imagined a squadron of Tornados being launched to intercept me if I continued onwards.

Amusingly enough, I did have an 'event' trying to fly across Upper Heyford, the American air base in Oxfordshire. I had only just acquired my licence and I was to take the aircraft from Denham in the south to Hinton-in-the-Hedges, a small airfield to the north. I drew a line on my map directly between the two and measured off where I should be every ten minutes. Happy with my plan I set off.

As I approached Upper Heyford, this American voice hailed me over the radio advising that I should immediately turn ninety degrees right. I replied that I had only just got my licence and that I was keeping to my planned route. His reply was immediate and urgent. "Turn right now or you will have two F1 elevens burning your arse." As you might imagine, I turned right immediately. I saw over my shoulder two steaks of light thundering towards the airfield.

I was now off course and not panicking but no longer confident that I could easily find my way. I have to tell you that I was delighted to hear the same American voice proposing that he would guide me by his radar to Hinton and wishing me a happy flying life.

I also managed once to find an airfield in the middle of the English Channel. I was flying across from England to visit my parents in Jersey, a route virtually due south. As I flew along, I noticed below me the Ark Royal aircraft carrier sailing majestically down the Channel. I descended and waggled my wings at it. Absolutely no response so I assumed that I hardly represented a threat to this beautiful fighting machine.

To supplement our income, we allowed a few chosen pilots who had been approved by Brian or Peter, to hire the aircraft. We only had one who seriously misbehaved. It was his engagement party and his friends in the pub teased him that, once married, his flying days would be seriously restricted. He took this as a challenge, left his friends, drove to the airfield at Denham took the Chipmunk out of the hanger and went back to fly some aerobatic manoeuvres over his friends in the pub.

He met two problems. He had not been able to get the headsets which were locked away in our hut and night was closing fast. There was not enough light for him to see clearly to land at Denham.

However, a few miles further south there was a well-lit airfield called Heathrow.

He flew there and landed and, surprised not to see any police or security people, taxied over to the perimeter fence, parked the aircraft so that its wing was against the fence, climbed over, hailed a taxi and went back to join his friends.

It seems that this was a quiet time for air traffic control at Heathrow so the person on duty had left station and gone for a coffee. It was just at this moment that the Chipmunk sneaked down the runway.

The following day I had promised my 12-year-old godson, Christopher, as a birthday present, a flight in the Chipmunk. We drove out to Denham. I opened the hanger doors to introduce Christopher to the Chipmunk.

No Chipmunk.

Instead, within seconds, we were surrounded by about three police cars. Having realised that the disappearance had nothing to do with us, it was the police who told us that the aircraft was at Heathrow sitting under the wing of an impounded 747 and the embarrassed authorities wanted me to fly it out. Christopher and I were driven by the police to Heathrow and met by a man of obvious authority who escorted us out to the aircraft.

I checked the aircraft and noticed that we did not have much fuel (Heathrow only had jet fuel and we used four star) so arranged with air traffic control to take off from their northern runway, the one closest to Denham being used that day for landing aircraft.

I settled Christopher into the rear seat and escorted by a FOLLOW ME van, we weaved our way out to the runway. Air Traffic asked me if I could get away between a landing Caravelle and a 747 that was approaching on their finals. I had a vision of the pilot of the 747 saying to himself 'get that bloody thing out of here. I have 400 on board and, after a long flight, the last thing I want is to have to go around again'.

Fortunately for him, I lined up, accelerated and lifted off turning north towards Denham. I couldn't understand why the aircraft kept wanting to gain height. It was only as I approached Denham that, in the excitement, I realised that I had not pulled my flaps up after take-off. No harm done but my hand ached from holding the stick forward over the few miles from Heathrow to Denham.

My aircraft partner Peter was at that time working on the William Hickey column of the Daily Express so we were item number three on the BBC news and the story was splashed over all the newspapers.

Peter was heard to mumble 'how was it that Peter had all the fun of flying it out of Heathrow?' I never asked what happened to the poor air traffic controller – a high price I would expect for one cup of coffee!

The pilot was banned from flying. However, I understood that, after ten years, he could apply for his licence again. I never knew whether he did or not nor indeed what his future bride thought about his exuberant behaviour.

Christopher still mentions it as the best birthday present ever and the adventure certainly stood me in good stead with professional pilots all of whom wanted to hear the story. This included, some years later, when I was flying on Concorde, the pilots inviting me up to the front to sit through the whole landing procedure from the moment the nose was lowered, through the descent, landing and taxing to the disembarkation point – a unique experience and all due to a young man's over enthusiastic response at an engagement party.

I was, at that time, guardian to my first two Jamaican children, Mark and Bruce Hart, nephews to Peter and Joan McConnell and sons of Tony and Sheila Hart. On occasional weekends, they would come and stay with me in Onslow Square and it was fun to be able to take them out to fly in the Chipmunk as well as to football matches, speedway and dog racing.

After one football match we were returning in the Underground and Mark and Bruce were chatting away in Jamaican patois much to the surprise of the other Jamaicans in the carriage. "How you speak patois so good?" demanded one of the locals. "We live in Montego Bay," was their reply which meant the rest of the journey was spent with all the Jamaicans chatting away in patois incomprehensible to me but obviously with joy to these new found countrymen.

What the news of this aviation escapade also did was to cause a call from our High Commissioner to come up and see him. Arthur Wint, Jamaica's High Commissioner in London at that time, was a very special man. He was the first Jamaican to win an Olympic gold medal, his success being at the 1948 Olympics. In fact, he won two gold and two silver medals, had trained as a doctor and was a personal friend of the Prime Minister. This, I knew. What I did not know was that during the war he had been a Spitfire pilot. He laughingly explained to me that at six feet four inches, his Spitfire had to be modified to accommodate his height. We had a most enjoyable half hour chatting about flying.

It is probably forgotten now but over 16,000 people, men and women, from the Caribbean volunteered for active service during the Second World War and over 40,000 joined various branches of the civilian war effort in the United States.

Working alongside us were two other Government agencies promoting Jamaica.

The first was the Jamaica Tourist Board responsible for tourism. The board was founded by our Chairman John Pringle and the current director, Norman Brunskill, was an Englishman of my age, both of us committed to the promotion of the island we found irresistible. The second was the JIDC or Jamaica Industrial Development Corporation. It was a one-man operation run by a Jamaican, Manny Henriques, who had served in the British navy during the war.

He told me once that he had been blessed with his posting during the war. He became captain of a mine sweeper and, instead of patrolling the icy and stormy coast of Great Britain, he had been posted to patrol the seas around Jamaica. As he said, he had had the great good fortune to patrol the waters of his own home island which had not been too seriously threatened by German U-boats.

Manny was definitely the more eccentric of us. His pet, which thankfully he kept at his home, was a python. When you visited him, he would answer the door with the python curled round his baldhead to keep his head warm, he claimed. He was a mine of information about Jamaican families and Jamaican businesses as his own family were the producers of Jamaica's best-known rum as well as being major players in the wine and spirit distribution business – Appleton Rum and Tia Maria, the coffee liqueur, being their best-known worldwide brands.

The three of us became great friends and Norman, his Trinidadian wife Valerie, and I and the girlfriend of the day would often holiday together in Jamaica.

Amongst our own domestic turmoil, in 1973 yet another war known as the Yom Kippur or October War broke out between Israel and a coalition of Arab states led by Egypt and Syria. In the early days of the war, my secretary Jennifer Henriques who happened to be Jewish, entered my office and asked for a favour. I replied, "Of course, as long as it doesn't concern my blood."

"Funny you should say that," she answered back, "but that is exactly what the favour does concern. There is a large demand for blood donations and my mother and I wondered if you would join us and come with us after work to the synagogue in St John's Wood where they are collecting blood. To be used for the wounded from both sides, I should hasten to add."

I agreed and that evening we drove up to St John's Wood and joined the queue waiting to enter the synagogue. Just as I was about to enter, my greengrocer Ivan came out of the door. I asked him how he had got on. He explained that he had some physical problem that did not allow him to be a donor. I jokingly replied that I would give an extra pint to take his place.

Sitting at the test desk, I noticed that both Jennifer and her mother were leaving. It came about the Jennifer had had polio and her mother cancer so they could not donate. This good, if lapsed, Catholic boy would now have to stump up four pints of blood for his Jewish friends. Fortunately, I was only required to give one but, having been told the story, I received the sincere gratitude from the amused nurse who took my blood.

The sequel to this story was that, thereafter, whenever I visited my greengrocer there was always a little extra seasonal present added to my grocery basket.

Jamaicans have a wonderful sense that everything Jamaican is the best in the world and I would be visited by Jamaicans hoping to sell their produce in Europe. One example will show this belief. This gentleman manufactured a range of kitchenware, mainly pots and pans. In a mixture of patois and standard English, he asked for my advice.

After questioning him, I discovered that he bought the raw materials from England, shipped them to Jamaica, where labour was no longer that cheap, manufactured the goods and then shipped them back to England.

He really couldn't understand why his product had to be more expensive than locally made ones and held to his belief that because they were from Jamaica, they had to be superior. It took me some time to convince him to concentrate on his local market.

The other characteristic that I love about Jamaicans is their enthusiasm and joy in living. Stewart, the younger brother of Peter and David McConnell, had come on holiday to London and had always wanted to visit Copenhagen. He invited me to join him for a weekend. I explained to him that I was not in his league for spending money to which he asked if I could pay for my airfare. I said yes, to which he replied, "Leave the rest to me."

We arrived in Copenhagen at about 5 pm just as all the secretaries and young female workers were leaving their offices. Stewart just spun like a top in the middle of the street fascinated by the bevy of blonde, Danish women that surrounded and swirled passed us. His only expression for the next few minutes was in patois – "Lord, a mercy. What a load of puss."

We arrived at our hotel to find that he had booked a suite and we spent a seriously enjoyable weekend night clubbing and touring the town.

I would also come to holiday at weekends with Peter and Gwen Tory. Peter's mother lived in Bermuda but kept a house in England for her occasional visits. Over the years that we spent together, she moved from a house in Kent, to a house near Henley and, finally to my favourite, at Enstone in Oxfordshire. Peter and Gwen looked after them for her and eventually sold their flat and moved into them.

Enstone had an old airfield at which we managed to rent part of a hanger and, when we needed to re-fuel, we would fly to Oxford airfield to fill up.

I spent nearly every weekend, certainly at their last two houses, with the Torys, the idea being that we would spend time flying together. This was not always possible. We would arrive from London on a Friday night and descend on the local pub for dinner at which we drank far too much so could not fly on the Saturday. On the Sunday, it poured with rain. Fortunately, this was not a frequent occurrence so we did get a good amount of flying time together.

During the summer months, when I had free time, I would climb up onto my roof with a radio tuned into air traffic control and sunbathe listening to the aircraft descending into

Heathrow. I could not help noticing rather an attractive woman sunbathing down in the garden. I determined to go and chat to her.

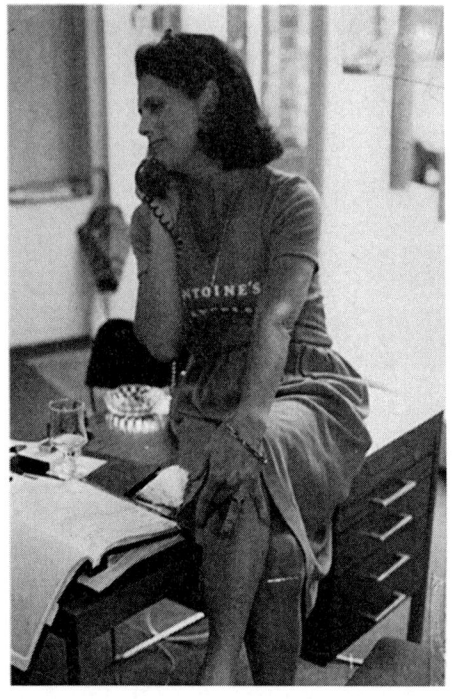

Penny, my first wife

Gathering up my courage one afternoon, I approached her with the classic opening line, "Hello, I'm Peter. I live just over there and I have noticed you sunbathing down here when I have been sunbathing up there. I suppose you wouldn't be interested in a cup of tea?"

She laughed (a good sign) and replied, "That is probably the worst chat up line, I have ever heard but, yes, why not."

Her name was Penny and she lived about four doors along from me, was divorced with two young sons at school at Charterhouse and worked as an estate agent. She was very attractive but had all the qualities of a classic Gemini woman. Like Alice, when she was good, she was very, very good and when she was bad, she was horrid. It seems that, should we get married, I would be the fourth to present her at the altar.

She was the daughter of an American mother and an English father. They, too, had divorced and the mother had married an Englishman, her father's best friend, and her father had married an American and now lived in Oyster Bay on Long Island.

Why meeting Penny reminded me that Annabel and I had vaguely kept in touch, I have no idea. She had married and then divorced Anthony, the son of the entertainer Max Bygrave. However, Annabel had now re-married Octavian, whom I had to admit was charming and very entertaining and they had asked me to be godfather to their second son. I found this a most pleasing offer as it was intended that we should at least keep in touch through our lives which we indeed did.

It was not long before Penny and I started living together dividing our time between her single bedroomed apartment and my three bedroomed one. Then, she had an extraordinary stroke of luck. The three bedroomed apartment opposite hers was owned by an elderly lady who approached Penny asking if she would swap apartments.

The old lady explained that she found it too difficult to manage the larger one and so would prefer a smaller one. Penny jumped at the chance and so became the owner of the lease for the larger apartment at no cost nor trouble to herself. We decided to live in her new apartment and rent out mine. I think my flatmates had seen the writing on the wall and both had found alternative living quarters so we parted amicably.

Colin, her elder son, had now left Charterhouse and had slipped into the world of drug taking though he did hold down a job as a sub-editor on a London newspaper.

Penny's biggest fear was that he might influence her younger son Anthony who was still at school. She became so embroiled in this fear that one Christmas evening when we were all together, she found Colin talking about drugs to Anthony in the kitchen and rang the police to report her own son as a drug user. The police arrived and took Colin aside for a search and for a lecture with the admonition that they now had his details on file.

It was not a particularly happy Christmas Day.

Thereafter, I did not have much to do with Colin nor, as far as I could see, did his mother, though I became close to Anthony and played the 'in loco parentis' role for his last year at school and after he left. It seemed that his father had remarried, had a second family and considered his duty over once he had paid for the boys' education.

It was in the Spring that I received a phone call from my mother. My father was ill, in hospital and she felt that I should come across to Jersey immediately. I flew over to visit my father and had the chance to talk to him just the once before he died the next day. Though our relationship had often been at arms-length in that we were never physically close for most of my life, I had enormous respect for him and enjoyment in his company.

I suppose he had spoilt me in that I had never wanted for money, though he also brought me up to know that we would never be millionaires. I am sure that the profligacy of his own parents and his family had a deep effect on him which he passed on to me.

He asked me if I had blown the money that he gave me when I was 21. I was able to reply that I could give him a cheque right now for it as I had always followed his advice and only used the interest. He admitted he was surprised but I thought I saw a look of approbation. I am not sure, therefore, whether he actually thought of me as a disappointment. I had not followed in his footsteps by joining the Professions and, as far as he was concerned, I lived a precarious life as a sort of West End hustler.

I do know, however, through a strange reason, that he was actually quite proud of me.

He had been firmly against me learning to fly and tried to convince me not to. Against his advice, I carried on and one day flew down to Bournemouth where my parents were holidaying. My father came out to the airfield to meet me and was waiting for me in an observation area.

Next to him were two young aircraft spotters, listening to the airfield radio. One said to the other, "Cor, there is a Chipmunk approaching. How I would love to fly in one of them. It's call sign is Golf Bravo Charlie Romeo Xray." My call sign. My father obviously could not resist so, with obvious pride, said to them, "That's my son, you know."

It was my mother who later told me this story so maybe he had found something about me of which he could be proud.

His ashes were buried in the rose garden of Jersey's crematorium, a small group of friends attending the wake. I could only stay for a couple of days to ensure that my mother would be alright. I was quite astonished to discover that she had never paid a bill in her life and that my father had run both their lives. Then, I realised that this was the way that many of their class and generation behaved. How different it was now in mine.

I managed to arrange for the family's accountancy firm to handle all her financial affairs and asked the Parish authorities to keep an eye out for her – a service that Jersey's Parishes were and still are happy to do.

Mother settled in enjoying the company of her maid Florrie, some three years older than my mother. I am not sure how much house work Florrie did but she was great company for my mother being a local girl and knowledgeable about all the local gossip.

To help in the garden, she had Peter Rabet (known to us as Peter Rabbit obviously) and her delight was to drive around the roads of Jersey steering down any road she felt like and pottering about in the garden. She seemed to be reasonably content with her widow's lot never complaining to me anyway and never openly bemoaning the loss of my father. After all, my mother came from a tough background – a true Durham lass.

I promised that I would come over often and returned to my life in London.

Looking back, I seemed to have had a talent for working myself out of jobs. On return from my father's funeral, I realised that there was not much more I could do for my Jamaican cigar manufacturers.

They had improved the quality of their cigars, their packaging and their marketing as well as their relationships with their UK importers. Sales were much better.

Their position as the second brand of hand-made cigars to Havanas was now reasonably well-established. As I said, there was not much more that I could do.

At the same time, my relationship with Arthur, my MD, was not good. We were two different characters. He seemed to me to be the model of a cold, puritanical Northern Irishman who didn't understand the essential spirit of our Jamaican employers and who, I felt, was either jealous or uncomfortable with the ease with which I communicated with both the high commission staff as well as my friends in Jamaica. We didn't actually come to blows but we began a series of unpleasant arguments which ended in my being, for the first time in my life, fired.

I have to admit that this came as a shock but, on reflection, understandable as I really had nothing to do and was not happy working for Arthur.

One of the Jamaican companies that I had got to know through Jamco offered me a job, oddly enough working for another Arthur, in a small office in the east of the City of London, an area completely alien to me but one I was looking forward to discovering.

The company was called Geddes Grant and my job was to set up the marketing of a range of mahogany furniture manufactured in Jamaica for importation into the English market. The range was called Jamaican Heritage and the designs were based on the mahogany furniture of the Jamaican great houses from the hey days of the plantocracy.

In this, I was fortunate. For my finals at Cranfield Business school, I had undertaken a consultancy project for two small furniture companies, one a manufacturer, the other a retailer of old pine furniture so I had some knowledge of the furniture industry in England.

We rented a warehouse in Camberwell in south east London and employed a salesman with whom I had worked when I consulted for my business school thesis. Between the three of us, we worked out a marketing programme which included a rather lavish but attractive brochure, took stands in various furniture exhibitions as well as trying to sell our wares directly to individuals or to furniture retailers.

We faced at least two problems. The first was with our manufacturer. Due to the policies of Michael Manley, the middle class had flooded out of Jamaica to homes in Canada or America and tourism had been devastated due to the island's growing reputation for violence. Those who remained were desperate for foreign exchange.

This meant that the factory wished to produce the largest and most expensive items whereas our customers, we soon found out, were only interested in smaller items, tables being the largest, chairs, side tables, coffee tables and nests of tables being the most preferred. Sometimes our orders for these items arrived in a container full of large cupboards and Welsh dressers – seriously frustrating.

The second problem was one that we had realised from the beginning which was that we were in a very specialised market. Our designs were traditional, in heavy dark mahogany whereas the general trend was for lighter more modern furniture. Despite this, we did find a small specialist market that gave us our income and justified our existence.

Life does have its wonderful lighter moments.

One day, I was taking the bus from Aldgate across the Thames to our warehouse in Camberwell. I was sitting in the top of the bus about three rows back from the front. In the front seat was a very large Jamaican woman. The bus conductor, also Jamaican, checked my ticket and moved towards the woman. Just as he reached her she gave an enormous belch. His reply was immediate.

"Lord 'a mercy, woman. If dat der one 'ad a turned down, it would have blown your drawers clean off." I had tears of laughter coursing down my cheeks. I still giggle to this day whenever I think of it – pure Jamaican humour.

I did find the east end of the City, or at least the part of it in which our office was situated, very grey. It had none of the charm or excitement of the West End in which I enjoyed working and playing. My favourite eating-place became an outside stall on a busy street called Tubby Isaac's – famous for jellied eels. It was one of the few places that I found the staff, often Tubby himself, interested in their customers and exuding bonhomie. A little sunshine found in a cloudy sky but, sadly, no longer in existence.

Further away and also Jewish was one of the best kosher restaurants in London. It was called Blooms and was founded in 1920 by Morris Bloom, an Ashkenazi Jew who had to flee one of the many pogroms in Russia. Sadly, the last Bloom's restaurant in Golders Green closed in 2010 and so ended its fame as the longest standing kosher restaurant in England.

During my two years with Geddes Grant, I had kept in touch with the largest of the English cigar importers, Hunters and Frankau. Perhaps, every three months I would have lunch with David, the managing director.

It was at one of these lunches that he asked me if I would be interested in returning to the world of hand-made cigars. It seemed that one of the brands they imported had been purchased by a Swiss company and the company had instigated a totally new way of storing and marketing their brand of cigars as well as creating a range of accessories carrying the brand name. The brand was Davidoff.

I have to admit I was excited as I had enjoyed the cigar trade. I was to be given virtually a free hand to introduce the brand into the UK. My salary was to be much the same as I earned at Geddes Grant but I was to benefit from a commission. This commission was agreed at 10% of my annual sales value and I also enjoyed a reasonable expense account.

I discussed this with Arthur who immediately understood my desire to leave and take up this new challenge. He kindly gave me his full support and I left to go to a new office close to Fleet Street where, of course, my good friend Peter worked and who quickly introduced me to the wine bar/restaurant El Vinos and his gaggle of disreputable gossip columnists.

My first step was to go to Basel, home to the head office, to meet my new colleagues led by Dr Ernst Schneider and his goffer Conrad who was to be my direct contact in Basel.

Whilst being introduced to the philosophy, methodology and product range which included not only cigars but also humidors, cigar cutters, cigarillos, pipes, pipe tobacco (Scottish being delicious with a beautiful aroma), matches and a lighter. There were also plans to introduce men's cosmetic products such as aftershave, cufflinks, key rings and other paraphernalia once the line had been established.

One morning, Conrad drove me to Geneva to introduce me to Zino Davidoff in his cigar retail emporium which had become famous to the townsfolk and visitors to Geneva. His father had started the business after he had fled Russia during yet another of the anti-Jewish pogroms and had started by making and selling cigarettes door to door.

He eventually opened a retail shop which was frequented by Russian and Jewish refugees, many of whom plotted the revolution sitting round the samovar, the centre piece of his shop. Zino proudly showed me an unpaid bill which he had framed and hung in the shop. It was for Havana cigars. The debtor was Lenin.

I was fascinated by how the Swiss, presumably all of them, ran their businesses. It was a far more hands-on affair than ever imagined by the British. I think at that time, Dr Schneider had 200 employees, employed over six floors of the office building.

Each day, he would drive into the basement garage and work his way up the building by going to each employee on each floor, shaking hands and enquiring after them and their family. I noticed how this generated a feeling of being part of the firm and approachable to the managing director.

It was a good lesson to learn should I ever run my own business.

Instead of travelling to and from Jamaica, I was now travelling to and from Basel. On one of my early visits, I was housed in a service flat and invited on my first night out to dinner with Dr Schneider and his wife.

The imposing frontage of the Davidoff shop in London's St James

They had invited an attractive German lady to make up the party who, I understood, had been Dr Schneider's secretary.

After coffee, our hosts left and the young lady and I went out on the town and, happily, shared breakfast. We enjoyed the following evenings of my visit together. I do not know to this day whether it was my inherent charm that appealed to the young lady or whether my host had arranged, even paid, for her attendance. Whichever, it was a thoroughly enjoyable visit which was never repeated on my future visits.

I now had to think how I would approach the cigar retailers who had been in business far longer than me, some of them for generations. It struck me that the only way to explain this actually dramatic and innovative method of selling cigars was to talk about the natural condition in which cigars were born and raised. This condition was the humidity that was endemic to Cuba and which leaves the tobacco naturally moist.

In practical terms, this would mean a small investment in converting a section of their cigar retail area into a humidifying area in which the cigars could be promoted on shelving and stored in their boxes beneath, preferably glass fronted.

Complementary to this was the opportunity for the retailer to promote the sale of home humidifiers which replicated the conditions of the humidifier by water containers within the humidor. Naturally, Davidoff could supply these as well – some made from beautiful woods selling for £1000 or more each.

By introducing this natural condition for the preservation and promotion of these cigars, I could justify its introduction and pave the way for a new, interesting and correct way to market hand-made cigars and my brand, Davidoff, was to lead the way.

I have to admit I was quite pleased with myself for putting this concept into practice so I set off to see how this would go down, first with the cigar retailers in London and, thereafter, through the United Kingdom.

In certain, seriously traditional outlets in London, I was quite firmly shown the door. The odd one even threatened to drop all cigar brands from my company if I insisted that they could only buy Davidoff from us if they introduced this, to them, ridiculous scheme. However, Harrods and two independent tobacconists Fox's and Sautter's of Mount Street were prepared to listen and did introduce the humidifying rooms. We had the start on which I could convince others to follow.

This began a regular tour that I undertook twice each year visiting cigar retailers throughout the country. I started by driving to Bristol, then Birmingham, Manchester and Carlisle. From there, I entered Scotland visiting Glasgow, Perth and Edinburgh. Finally, back down the east coast of England including Newcastle, York and Cambridge.

One of the perks of this journey was that I would stay in the best hotels I could find in order to see how they served their cigars, even if they did not actually serve them.

One of the promotional tasks that I took upon myself each year was to spend a pre-Christmas fortnight as a Davidoff salesman in the newly constructed humidifying room in the ground floor cigar department of Harrods department store. This took me back to my days as a Brown and Polson rep and I thoroughly enjoyed it. This was the time when the wealthy Arabs swarmed into London and were extremely generous about spending their money.

My modus operandi was to offer potential customers a Davidoff cigarillo which, in those days, they could smoke immediately and then talk to them about the delights of Davidoff's real cigars. I, of course, included cigar cutters and humidors and often the amount they spent would amount to two or three thousand pounds.

One particular customer not only spent close to ten thousand pounds but also slipped two fifty-pound notes into my top pocket as a thank you. Both the department buyer and myself were delighted with the success that we both claimed to have achieved.

At the end of my first year, I was summoned to David, the managing director's office. The subject was my year end salary and commission. He explained that with my commission set at 10% of annual turnover, I was earning more than him.

The arrangement would have to be changed and I would henceforth receive 10% of the profit on sales not turnover. There was not much I could do but agree.

He was not amused when at the end of the second year, I was again summoned to his office to be told that I had again earned more than he did. This time, I explained that the arrangement could not be changed but that he should be delighted that my sales actually benefitted him as well as me. The arrangement was left as it was.

A few months later, I was again summoned to the managing director's office to be introduced to an Iranian gentleman called Edward Sahakian. Edward and his family were one of the many Iranians that had to flee Iran after the Revolution that removed Shah Pahlavi and introduced the anti-west Islamic Republic of Ayotollah Ruhollah Khomeini.

His proposition was that he wanted to open a Davidoff retail shop in the west end of London and required us, as Davidoff's sole UK distributor, to facilitate and support his proposition.

We could see no reason why not as we bore no financial risk and we would gain a flagship Davidoff retailer in the West End. Admittedly, this would be in competition with our other West End retailers but that was a risk worth taking.

I was appointed to be his wing man as far as the Davidoff organisation was concerned.

Edward had employed a rather attractive architect called Albena and had arranged a lunch for us all to meet each other. I was seated next to Albena and was merrily chatting her up when she introduced me to the man sitting on her other side.

This was her husband Anthony, employed by Edward as his estate expert. Despite this inauspicious start, the three of us became very great friends.

Anthony proved to be a fellow golfer and one day I took him to play at the Berkshire Golf course. After our game, we were having a drink in the bar when Virgilio the steward approached me to ask whether I was driving back to London. On replying yes, he asked if I would give a lift to two other golfers who had been stranded without transport. I explained that I only had a Mini but they were very welcome to sit in the back.

We were introduced to two actors Michael Medwin and Sean Connery, then at the height of his fame as James Bond. It was quite an unforgettable drive back to London with Sean Connery's knees supporting my head. It seemed that James Hunt was to have been their driver but he had received a phone call from a girlfriend who lived nearby and had left them in the lurch. I have to admit they were both charming and grateful.

Anthony, quite quickly considering, found the perfect site for the Davidoff shop on the corner of St James Street and Jermyn Street and the work began on preparing the shop designed to be a Mecca for those who loved smoking and smoking related products.

Its entrance made the corner of the two streets with full sized plate-glass windows displaying the brightly lit and luxurious interior. Above the entrance were inscribed, in large, impressive letters, the word Davidoff and above the side windows, in large letters, the words Davidoff Fine Cigars. Just to ensure that any passer-by was in no mistake where they were, each window was etched with the word Davidoff in a large circle.

It was both striking and enticing, a well-designed shop and a pleasing edition to the boutique shops in this part of the West End of London.

I had now settled in with Penny and had let out my apartment to a rather exotic and, seemingly reasonably wealthy Italian. He was also very attractive and there was no doubt that Penny found him interesting.

To this day, I am not sure whether they had an affair but the possibility caused an enormous strain in our relationship, finally to such a degree, that we broke up and I moved into a small apartment in Wetherby Gardens, further out in South Kensington.

My new apartment was just what I needed. Two of my friends from the Berkshire Golf Club, Simon and Alastair, both had apartments in the same house, one below me and one above. Alastair was married to Caroline whose golfing prowess was just that bit better than mine so we often played together on a Sunday before the traditional golf club Sunday lunch.

Simon was ten years younger than me, a bachelor, who had a selection of very pretty girl friends, one Maiken having been a Playboy centrefold and you don't get much better than that. She was a very attractive Scandinavian blonde but charming, very natural and she became a great friend to all of us.

I had met Simon some years before in Jersey. I was staying one post-Easter weekend with my parents when I received a telephone call saying a visiting golf team, called the Beefeaters, was one short and could I play for them.

I did and at lunch the first day, I sat with Simon who was to be my partner in the afternoon foursomes. We were introduced after lunch to a creation of the steward's own invention called a Starboard Light. This was a mixture of Crème de Menthe, gin and vodka. We must have had two or three of them because when we teed up after lunch, we could not see a white ball below us, everything was green. We took alternate shots but were still standing on the tee after at least three attempts each to hit the ball. As you might imagine, we lost that match.

It then turned out that Simon lived near me in London and this started my relationship with the Berkshire Golf Club and also my membership of the golfing society, the Beefeaters, which was based around the Berkshire. The naming of the golf society, the Beefeaters, had nothing to do with either the gin or the guardians of the Tower of London. It had started by three founder members who, just after the war when everything was rationed, would play golf against a fellow member, a butcher.

They would play for a sirloin of beef which they would enjoy that evening at their golf club.

They decided to form a golfing society, called it the Beefeaters and it is still going strong to this day. Having been an enthusiastic member for 40 years, I have at last qualified to be a member of its Senior Common Room.

During this period, I had kept in touch with Penny's younger son Anthony or, more exactly, he kept in touch with me. I would get reports from him that his mother regretted our break up and, eventually, would I consider seeing her again.

What was interesting was that Peter and Gwen did not like her at all though Anthony and Albena did. She had that sort of polarised effect on people.

There is no doubt that I was still in love with her and found her very exciting and sexy company. She was one of those striking women that people look at whenever they enter a room and, if I am truthful, was the first woman to replace Annabel as the girl of my dreams.

One problem was that one of the other people who did not like her was my mother. Penny had stupidly told my mother that she had been switched to safe and that two sons were her desired quantity in the breeding department. Obviously, this did not go down well with my mother who had, for years, been hinting to me that a grandchild was her greatest desire. Penny's suggestion that she could be a grandmother to her two sons did not amuse my mother.

Of course, it would happen that my mother was staying with me in my small two bedroomed apartment when I agreed with Anthony that I would like to see his mother again.

Our reunion was so enthusiastic that we decided to get married. My mother did not bear the news well and Peter invited me out to lunch to convince me not to marry her.

However, I was determined and so we were married at Chelsea Registry Office with, at least, my mother (who had threatened not to join us) and our friends accepting the 'fait accompli' and Penny and I set off to America and Jamaica for our honeymoon.

I was now 40 and this just seems an appropriate moment to end this account of my life to date. It is a period that I look back on and consider to be my formative years in which I had been trying to establish a life that was not the norm for most of my friends who seemed to be content with a more staid lifestyle – a style very much programmed from their school days and their English social background.

This just did not happen for me and it is why I titled this autobiography 'The Growing Pains of a Colonial Boy' because the more I thought about my life, I realised that I was in fact an outsider. I was a Colonial Boy.

The End